CATHERINE AND WILLIAM ODELL

The First Human Right

A Pro-Life Primer

OUR SUNDAY VISITOR, INC.

To Evelyn and Albert Odell and Marcella and Robert Anthony, our parents, who were our first and best Life teachers. To our friends in the pro-life movement, especially in Indiana, who work selflessly to share the message that life was created to be loved, defended, and celebrated.

THE FIRST HUMAN RIGHT
Copyright © by Our Sunday Visitor, Inc. 1983
200 Noll Plaza   Huntington, Indiana 46750
All rights reserved
Library of Congress Catalog Card No. 82-61466
International Standard Book Number 0-87973-620-8
Printed in the United States of America
90 89 87 86 85 84 83 5 4 3 2 1

Contents

Preface

It was Monday, January 22, 1973. Late in the morning, in Washington, D.C., the United States Supreme Court handed down a ruling that would make each future January 22nd the anniversary of an unprecedented tragedy.

On that day, the nation's highest court uniformly legalized abortion for all fifty states and for all stages of pregnancy. The war against mankind's most defenseless members took off in earnest. In the next ten years in the U.S., more than 13.5 million unborn children would be killed.

This "decade of destruction" has prompted the writing of this book. After many years of involvement with pro-life issues, we are well acquainted with the "hard" questions and with those most frequently asked. We have posed them in these pages, along with others that should be asked. Our book is not intended to be a complete study of the abortion controversy here in the U.S. Nor does it attempt to say everything that can be said about euthanasia and infanticide, those attacks upon innocent human life that followed so soon after the assault on the unborn had begun. We have attempted to provide the information needed for a fundamental grasp of the life issues.

The question-and-answer format of our book will, we hope, be useful for people of all ages who want to know more about the most critical challenge of our times—the challenge to the first human right.

—Catherine and William Odell

Introduction

In the course of my pro-life involvement, I have consistently felt the need for a book like this one: a pro-life primer that details all the current issues and distills all the essential facts into one easy-to-read volume.

I think that there are many people who hold back from active commitment to the pro-life struggle because they doubt their mastery of the basic information. For such persons as these, as well as for those who have long been involved in the pro-life movement, the Odells have provided a well-organized, complete, and very clear sourcebook.

It has seemed to me, likewise, that many of us assume that the human-life issues are too large and too complicated to allow us to reach the definite convictions that are the foundation for active involvement. In a pluralistic society such as ours, amidst the blizzard of contrary opinions, our own certainties tend to be undermined by constant challenge. In times like ours, a book like this one is desperately needed. It brings clarity out of confusion and leaves the reader with firm grounds for conviction. By its simple and clear exposition of facts, it invites the reader to active dedication.

Our country now stands at the crossroads of the most important choice we as a nation have ever had to make. The subject is human life. Will we renew our dedication to the traditional reverence and respect for each and every human life? Will we regard each human life as an image and likeness of God? Will we accept each human person as someone sent into this world by God with a unique message and a unique love-challenge for the human family? Or will we opt for a "quality of life" ethic that insists on a case-by-case evaluation of every human being's right to exist? Such an ethic, already being propagandized with great determination, demands that the "quality" of every human life must meet certain standards if that person is to be welcomed as a member of the human family. The penalty for failure to measure up to these standards is death.

The judicial system of our country has already legalized the killing of the unborn. This system is now in the process of rationalizing and legalizing the killing of those babies born with physical or mental deficiencies. There is likewise a great propaganda effort already launched to promote euthanasia of the helpless or suffering elderly.

From every quarter, we are being told that we can and must decide which lives are and which lives are not worth living. The secular humanists, in their *Manifesto*, tell us that there is no God. It seems to follow, on their logic, that we must regard ourselves as gods. If anyone poses a problem for us, or interferes with our personal pursuit of "the good life," that person's life must be thought of as a problem to be eliminated. We must tidy up the stage of human drama, denying the right of participation to those whose existence burdens us and asks of us an unselfish devotion.

I am personally very grateful for books like this one that summon us back to our senses. Someone has said that the spirit of secular humanism has changed all the price tags on the realities of the world. Such a spirit has placed high value on the trivial and cheapened the things that God and our human family have always held to be precious, such as human life. Catherine and William Odell have done us all a great service. They have calmly and cogently handled all the hard questions and, by their clear and direct answers, put the right price tags back in place. We are in their debt.

John Powell, S.J.
LOYOLA UNIVERSITY, CHICAGO

The Unborn's Odyssey

When does human life begin?
Scientists identify the first moment of human life as that instant when a sperm cell unites with an ovum, or egg cell. Prior to this moment, the ovum was inching its way toward or through the womb in just the same manner as does each of the approximately 400 ova released by the ovaries during a woman's reproductive years. As of the moment of fertilization, however, this ovum, or egg cell, takes on an entirely different destiny. The sperm penetrates the ovum, and fifteen thousand genes from the nucleus of the sperm and another fifteen thousand from the nucleus of the ovum form a unique combination that is nothing less than a new human being at the earliest stage of his or her life.

Though very small, this new life is nonetheless, and undeniably, a brand-new member of the human species. Like every other human being who has ever lived, he carries the basic chromosome structure (normally, 46 chromosomes) that is both his membership card in the human race and a blueprint for his future growth and development.

How big is this brand-new human being?
The newly conceived human weighs only 0.0004 mg and measures only 0.1 mm in diameter. Smaller at first than the period at the end of this sentence, the new human immediately begins to grow at a phenomenal rate.

If all the cells of the mother's body are living cells, what is so special about the fertilized ovum?

All the other living cells in the mother's body bear the genetic code of the mother. The fertilized ovum has a genetic (chromosomal) identity entirely distinct from that of the mother and that of the father. If nature is allowed to take its usual course, the single fertilized cell will grow and subdivide. Eventually the child's body will consist of literally millions of cells. At birth, this child who was once one cell, is an appealing armful, a baby boy or girl.

What is the difference between conception (fertilization) and implantation?

Conception marks the actual beginning of a new human life. *Implantation* refers to the process by which the new human life takes up residence in the uterus (or womb). After conception occurs (usually in a fallopian tube), the fertilized ovum moves down the tube, a journey of three to four days. Once in the uterus, the new life, now a cluster of cells called a morula (though still no bigger than a grain of sand), burrows into the soft lining of the uterus and derives nourishment from the uterine lining. About twelve days after fertilization, implantation in the uterus is complete.

Since so many fertilized ova do not survive long enough to become implanted, shouldn't implantation be considered the actual starting point of a human life?

The mortality rate for fertilized ova is high during the first weeks after conception. As high as fifty percent, by some estimates. Yet there is no scientific basis for identifying the starting point of human life as other than the moment of conception. Prior to that moment, the new life did not exist; from that moment, the tiny conceptus began a life's career in the very same way that all of us did. It is conception, not implantation, that marks the start of a new human life, regardless of how brief or how long that life may be.

What happens during the first week of human life, following conception?

During the very first week of life, the fertilized ovum moves down the fallopian tube to the uterus (womb) and becomes implanted there. What began as a single cell has grown to about a hundred cells in just one week. This cell mass, which now resembles a cluster of berries, is called a morula ("mulberry," in Latin). Until implantation, the hollow-centered cluster is still smaller than a grain of sand. As the morula begins to absorb nutrients from the womb, growth is much more rapid.

At least during the first few weeks, isn't the new human life like an appendix or tumor that can justifiably be removed if the mother wishes?

Though fragile and tiny during the first few weeks of life, the new human being is not just another part of the mother's body. Nature provides the new being with a separate circulatory system that is attached by means of the umbilical cord to the mother. The new creature has his own intrauterine space capsule too—the amniotic sac. But the clearest evidence that a *new* human life exists is that each of the cells of the conceptus possesses a unique genetic code that is different from that of either parent.

Saying that a baby is biologically human doesn't mean that he or she is fully human, does it?

To be biologically human is to have a genetic alphabet (genetic code) that spells *Homo sapiens*. To look for other measuring sticks for humanness—age, physical or mental development, consciousness, ability to relate emotionally, or anything else—is to fail to address the question of what species that living being belongs to from the beginning.

How does the unborn child develop during the first month?
During the first month in the life of the unborn child, cells multiply very rapidly and begin to take on specialized functions. By the twenty-eighth day after conception, tiny arm and leg buds have sprouted. Brain, spinal cord, and rudimentary vertebrae are present in the little *embryo* (from the Greek word meaning "to swell"), which ends the month measuring one fourth of an inch in length. Beginnings of eyes, thyroid gland, lungs, stomach, liver, kidneys, and intestines are also present. Ever since the twenty-fifth day, the heart, which is very large in proportion to the rest of the body, has been beating sixty-five times a minute to pump blood through the embryo's body.

What developments occur during the unborn's second month?
By the seventh week after conception, the child's nose, ears, eyes, lips, and tongue are present, and milk teeth are forming in the baby's gums. Though the unborn's arms measure no more than an eighth of an inch at this time, hands, complete with fingers and thumbs, are already present. The lower limbs, though slower to grow, have recognizable knees, ankles, and feet. During this second month of life, eye pigmentation, nose shaping, and the formation of the inner ear occur. The child's eyelids now nearly cover his eyes. Embryologists know exactly what new developments to look for on any given day of the child's second month. They know, for instance, that by the forty-eighth day, bone cells will have begun to replace cartilage. The baby grows about one millimeter each day during this second month.

What happens during the third intrauterine month?
Between the eighth and twelfth weeks of life, the unborn

baby becomes much more active. Skeletal structure, muscles, and nervous system are developing rapidly during this time. The child, now called a *fetus* (from the Latin for "young one," "little one"), can kick, fan his toes, make a fist, move his wrists, turn his head, open his mouth, and swallow considerable quantities of the amniotic fluid that surrounds him—but there is no danger that the baby will drown. This swallowing is thought to help in the development of the lungs. The baby's oxygen is supplied through the umbilical cord by the mother.

Toward the end of the third month, the little human is recognizably male or female. Toenails and fingernails have begun to form. Fingerprints develop, as do the vocal cords that the baby will one day use to make his wishes known.

What developments take place during the fourth month of life in the womb?

During the fourth month, the unborn child makes great gains in body size. Having begun the month at about three inches in length, he will grow another five inches during the four-week period. His weight, meanwhile, increases sixfold. Even at that, by the end of the month, the fetus will weigh only six to eight ounces. The mother often begins to show her pregnancy in the fourth month. She may begin to feel her young one kicking.

The baby's heart pumps about twenty-five quarts of blood through his body each day. Through the placenta, the child receives nutrients from the mother's bloodstream. (The placenta is an organ made up of tissue and blood vessels, which develops and "takes root" in the uterine lining.) Carbon dioxide and other wastes are removed from the baby's bloodstream by the placenta. Connected to the umbilical cord, the placenta provides the unborn child an uninterrupted supply of nourishment. In the same way, however, alcohol, nicotine, and other drugs can enter the child's system from the mother's body.

What of the development of the unborn through the fifth and sixth months?

After the halfway point in the journey toward birth is reached, the unborn child is already responding to events *outside* his mother's body. Loud noises and even bright lights can startle him. The mother will sometimes notice that her child has hiccups. The child spends some of his intrauterine time sucking his thumb or holding on to the umbilical cord. Happily, the child in the womb often uses his mother's rest time to take his naps. A creamy substance called vernix protects the child's skin from the amniotic waters. As the child completes the second trimester of life in the womb, he is about twelve inches long and weighs about a pound and a half. By this time, his lungs are well developed. Should he be born prematurely, the baby has a fairly good chance of surviving.

Doesn't 'quickening' occur around the fifth or sixth month?

Quickening is an old-fashioned term that refers more to what the mother is feeling, really, than to what the child in the womb is doing. The original meaning of *quick* is "alive." When a mother first became aware of the baby's movements within her body, she would say that the baby had "quickened." In fact, the baby had been up to a variety of intrauterine gymnastics for quite some time.

At what stage is the baby capable of surviving outside the mother's womb?

Today's answer to this question may be out of date tomorrow. Viability, or the capability of surviving outside the womb, is not so much a measurement of the baby's development as it is of the medical equipment and expertise of those attending the birth. As medical expertise grows, the survival rate for infants as young as twenty-one weeks continues to increase.

What is the baby like in the seventh month?

By the end of the seventh month, the child weighs about two and a half pounds. Fat has accumulated beneath the child's previously transparent skin, which is thicker now and somewhat glossy. The child may have some hair on his head now; but much of the downy-fine hair, called lanugo, that had grown on his arms, legs, and back falls out. In the seventh month, too, there is a buildup of antibodies that will afford the child protection against diseases after he has left the protection of the womb.

At what point can the baby see, taste, hear, et cetera?

While still in the womb, the child can and does use all the senses, perhaps with the exception of the sense of smell. In the seventh month, the eyes are reopening, and the unborn child gives every appearance of being able to see as well as hear. The child's reactions to strong lights and loud noises outside the mother's body demonstrate that the uterus is neither entirely dark nor completely silent.

Experiments have shown that by the eighth or ninth week of pregnancy the child in the womb will swallow more frequently if the amniotic fluid in which he floats is sweetened by injection, and less frequently if the fluid is given a bitter taste. Introducing pain stimuli—sharp instruments, heat, pressure—will elicit avoidance responses from the unborn child as early as the fourth month of intrauterine life.

When do the unborn child's major body-systems begin to function?

All of the unborn child's major systems—circulatory, respiratory, nervous, digestive, excretory—are present by the eighth week of life and are functioning well by the eleventh. In the womb, the child "breathes" amniotic fluid instead of oxygen, receiving necessary oxygen through the umbilical cord. Some of the child's wastes are removed through the cord. The unborn child's heart has been at work since the third week of life. In the seventh week after conception, electrical brain-wave patterns can already be monitored. During the third month of life, nerve and muscle connections have developed sufficiently to allow the child a wide variety of movements.

What happens during the child's last two months in the womb?

During the last six to eight weeks in the watery world of the womb, the baby gains four to five pounds and is now so strong that his (or her) best kicks can knock a book off mother's lap. Since there is no longer enough room to do somersaults, the infant is most likely to rest in a head-downward position in the womb. That is now the child's most comfortable position, for the head is the heaviest part of his body.

During the final weeks of residence in the womb, the child receives immunities to certain diseases through the placenta (after birth, the child will receive additional immunities from his mother's milk).

Just as the cessation of heartbeat and brain function signals death, shouldn't their beginnings mark the start of life?

No. The life process begins the moment ovum and sperm unite to create a new and genetically unique human life. The life activities of growth and development that immediately follow prepare the way for the development of the heart and the beginning of brain function.

What activates the birth process?

About a week before the end of the normal 266-day pregnancy, the placenta ceases to supply food to the unborn child and begins to deteriorate. Medical science does not yet completely understand all the factors involved in this first stage of the birth process. Scientists generally believe that the onset of labor (abdominal contractions) is electrochemically triggered by some kind of signal from the cramped child in the womb.

The uterus narrows, and the baby's body straightens toward the birth canal, normally in a head-downward position. The five plates of the child's skull are squeezed together, even to overlapping, so as to contract the size of the head. Intense muscular contractions of the uterus move the baby down into the birth canal. A 100-pound propulsive force sends the child out into an environment that is noisy, bright, dry, and considerably cooler. As the umbilical cord is exposed to air, circulation is cut off from the cord's blood vessels. The baby's lungs inflate with air, a process sometimes stimulated by a sharp slap on the back that causes the baby to cry. Life outside the womb has just begun; but the baby, who has been living in the womb for about nine months, merely continues his life where he can be seen.

Will a 'test-tube baby' develop in the same way as a baby conceived naturally?

Test-tube babies are conceived as a result of the union of ovum and sperm cells, as are all babies, but under unusual circumstances. Because of blockage of, or damage to, the fallopian tubes, through which the ova pass into the uterus, a woman may be functionally sterile even though she ovulates normally. A test-tube-baby procedure is a technique by which one of her own ova may be fertilized by sperm from her husband.

In this procedure, ripe ova are removed from a woman's ovary with a needle. The physician is able to see the much-magnified ovary by means of an optical aid called a laparascope, which is inserted into the woman's body. Because her ovaries have earlier been stimulated by the introduction of hormones, they release a number of ova instead of one, which is the normal number.

The ova, or eggs, are placed in a glass dish containing blood serum and nutrients. Sperm are added to the dish. Once fertilization occurs, a likely-looking conceptus is transferred to another dish. After about six days, the fertilized egg cell has become a tiny cluster of cells. This cluster is then inserted in the mother's uterus, which has been treated with hormones so that it will respond just as if conception had occurred in the normal manner.

Since 1978, when Louise Brown, the world's first test-tube baby, was born in England, the number of test-tube babies has been increasing quickly.

Why do some object to the 'test-tube baby' procedure?

Producing test-tube babies involves a selection process that destroys many lives in their first hours. Only one of about twenty fertilized eggs is successfully transplanted to the womb. The others fail to implant, are lost, or are deliberately destroyed. Once the baby begins growing in the womb, the woman's amniotic fluid is tested to see if the child is normal. If not, the child is likely to be aborted.

Robert Edwards and Patrick Steptoe, the British physicians who developed the procedure, have also decided to try to develop an embryo-donor bank, which would freeze "surplus" embryos and donate them to infertile women—with the permission of the donors. Dr. Edwards has admitted that in other experiments on seventeen test-tube embryos, all of them died within five days.

In September of 1982, some of Britain's test-tube mothers publicly expressed outrage over experimentation done on embryos. One of them, who said that she was grateful for a procedure that had given her a baby boy, described the experiments on living human beings as "morally terrible."

Why Abortion?

What does the term 'abortion' mean?
Abortion is the expulsion of a child from the womb. When this occurs spontaneously, it is called a miscarriage. The word *abortion* is commonly used to designate deliberately induced abortions. Abortion advocates make use of a variety of euphemisms to camouflage the brutal reality of the act: pregnancies are "terminated" or "interrupted" in order to remove the "products of conception" from the womb. Perhaps the classic example of pro-abortion doublespeak is the labeling of abortion as "retrospective fertility control." The fact that every abortion takes a baby's life is systematically ignored by the vocabulary of those who support abortion.

Should a 12-year-old girl be forced to bear a child if she should happen to become pregnant?
The sad scenario of the young pregnant girl is sometimes offered as evidence that abortion must be retained as a legal option. It is objected that a mother can hardly be expected to care for a child when she herself is a child. Abortion backers insist that, in addition to the psychological strain on the child-mother, the physiological stress of carrying a baby to term is unjustifiably difficult for the still-immature female body. But the fact that a young girl is not really well prepared to bear and rear a child does not amount to a proof that abortion is the answer to her difficulty.

Doctors know that abortion poses an enormous threat to

the physical health of an adolescent girl—and that there is serious danger of psychological damage to the youngster as well, sometimes setting in years after the abortion was performed.

The girl of twelve may feel relatively little concern for the life of her unborn child. Yet that same girl, several years later, may be psychologically devastated by the vivid realization that she has destroyed her own child.

Even though the child-mother is too immature to care for her baby, there are many married couples ready and eager to adopt an infant.

Isn't pregnancy often the result of rape?

Pregnancy as a result of rape is very rare. Dr. C. Everett Koop, surgeon general for the Reagan administration, referring to studies done in Minnesota and Pennsylvania, stated that of five thousand rape cases reported during a given period, not one pregnancy resulted. All studies done to date agree that rape rarely results in pregnancy. The reasons are many. Typically, a woman can become pregnant only on about three to five days during each menstrual cycle. Further, there is a high rate of sexual dysfunction among rapists. In addition, the victim may be using a contraceptive, already pregnant, or infertile because of age or other conditions.

Isn't abortion justified when the pregnancy is the result of rape?

Medical and law-enforcement personnel and sometimes even the families of rape victims are often insensitive to the suffering of a woman who has been raped. Sometimes the victim is made to feel that she was at fault. If a woman does become pregnant as a result of having been raped, she may be tempted to take her rage out on the child. In such cases, the woman, who was an innocent victim, becomes the victimizer—of her unborn child. The child exists and has committed no crime. He or she is completely innocent, a child of God, not responsible for the manner of his conception, and in no way deserving of the death penalty.

Victims of rape should be aware that pregnancy can be avoided by seeking treatment *immediately* after rape. Such treatment is necessary to prevent venereal disease and to deal with other possible injuries.

Isn't abortion justified when pregnancy results from incest?

Incest has always been taboo (forbidden) in most cultures. Sexual activity between unmarried related individuals is also illegal in most states and countries. Yet incest does occur, a telling symptom of unhealthy family relationships. Because society does hold incest in horror, abortion is commonly advised when pregnancy results.

Pregnancy resulting from incest rarely is discovered until sometime in the second trimester (three-month period). By then, the chances that abortion will involve medical complications for the mother are much increased.

Incest results in pregnancy only rarely; and professionals who deal with such situations have found that abortion of the unborn child does further damage to the family involved. The pregnancy can help the girl and her family face the incestuous situation, whereas abortion is a way of not dealing with an unhealthy state of affairs.

The unborn child cannot be considered to have forfeited his right to life merely because his origin was socially abhorrent. Once *any* child is conceived, his life and future deserve to be protected.

Can abortion to save the life of the mother be justified?

Therapeutic abortion—that is, an abortion to save the life of the mother—naturally wins more support than any other type of abortion. Nonetheless, pregnancies that truly threaten the life of the mother are very rare indeed. According to the National Center for Health Statistics, in 1980 the number of deaths from pregnancy-related causes was 6.8 per

100,000. That means one maternal death out of 14,706 pregnancies! With today's improved medical technologies, pregnancy is a safe experience. As statistically rare as maternal death is, such a death sometimes is the result, not of pregnancy itself, but of cancer, thrombo-embolic disease, or heart disease that happens to coincide with pregnancy.

In those very rare cases in which the mother's life is threatened by her pregnancy, every effort should be made to preserve the lives of both the mother and the baby. One case is cancer of the uterus. Another is an ectopic pregnancy, which develops in the fallopian tube and eventually ruptures the tube, causing hemorrhage. Doing what is necessary to save the woman's life will result in the loss of the child's life, but the intent is not to kill the child. In such cases, the child would have died before natural birth anyway.

Some proponents of abortion freely use the phrase "therapeutic abortion" to include abortion in cases of rape or incest, abortion of an impaired child, and abortion to preserve the mother's health. Such usage renders the phrase meaningless.

Aren't some women coerced into having abortions?
In interviews with women who have undergone abortions, one quite often hears "had to." Pressures—subtle and less than subtle—are often brought to bear on these women. Frequently they see themselves as victimized by outside forces. Sometimes pressure comes from a spouse who bemoans the financial havoc another child would supposedly wreak upon the family. Or an employer may hint that the job is too tough to be managed by a pregnant woman. Sometimes parents communicate, wordlessly perhaps, to their unmarried minor daughter, who is pregnant, that their sense of humiliation is a terrible burden for them. The girl's boyfriend may threaten to end their relationship if she doesn't "get rid of it."

Sometimes there is no one near to share the burdens and the joys of a new life. Abortion is a destructive act, and many women would not seek it as a solution if they were not caught up by a sense of helplessness.

Isn't it better to allow abortion when the child is unwanted?
It is an unfounded presumption that a child unwanted at
conception will be unwanted at birth. There is a persistent
presumption that if an unwanted child is allowed to be born,
he or she will later be abused. Abortion, therefore, is
presumed to reduce the number of cases of child battering. In
fact, incidences of child beating have increased during our
era of abortion-on-demand, and most battered children were
wanted children.

Every abortion is an act of agression against a helpless innocent. Thirteen million such acts since the Supreme Court
struck down virtually all restrictions against abortion-on-demand have fostered the attitude that children are a throw-
away commodity. The value of children thus diminished, the
sense of a duty to care for them has also diminished. Existing
children in families in which abortions have occurred may
well wonder if they were wanted—and if they will one day
become unwanted. They won't buy the explanation that the
abortion was done "out of love."

Planned Parenthood and other organizations have extolled
the virtue of making sure that "every child [is] a wanted
child." But to ground a child's right to exist on someone
else's wanting him is irrational, and to do so certainly doesn't
prepare a parent for the constant giving that child rearing demands.

**Isn't abortion justified when the parents know the child will
be handicapped?**
A physically or mentally handicapped child is a human being
as truly as is a normal child, and no less loved by his Creator.
He is not without value. A Down's syndrome child, for instance, can become a contributing member of the family and
of society. Like any child, he or she needs love, a sense of
belonging, a chance to express himself, and an opportunity
to achieve success in those activities that are within his range
of competence. By striving to provide for their child's needs,
the parents become better human beings.

Medical science is on the threshold of being able to do much for the defective child in the womb. Intrauterine treatment can correct problems or alleviate them so that the child can live a reasonably normal life. Yet amniocentesis, a method of detecting defects in the unborn child, is often used in a destructive way. When a physically or mentally handicapped infant is "identified," a recommendation to abort commonly follows.

What is amniocentesis?

Amniocentesis is a prenatal diagnostic technique that can determine whether the unborn child is afflicted with serious handicaps. A sample of the amniotic fluid is withdrawn by means of a needle from the mother's womb, and the discarded fetal cells in the fluid sample are tested. Down's syndrome, cystic fibrosis, Tay-Sachs disease, sickle-cell anemia, neural-tube defect, and other problems can be diagnosed by this method. Yet diagnosis based on amniocentesis is not always accurate, and there have been cases in which the misdiagnosis of a healthy child is discovered only after an abortion has been performed.

Though amniocentesis has great potential for treating the diseased child in the womb, it has all too often been used as a preliminary step toward abortion instead. Sadly, the ability of medical science to discover the sex of the child, before the pregnancy is far advanced, has prompted some parents to abort children of the "wrong" sex.

Isn't abortion justified when a woman has been using birth control carefully but conceives anyway?

From time to time, some women find that their contraceptive efforts have failed and that they are pregnant. Even the best contraceptives protect only 98 or 99 percent of the time. Women who find themselves pregnant because of "contraceptive failure" often say they have a right to choose abortion. "We weren't responsible for this child. The IUD was responsible," insisted one woman who chose abortion to "erase the mistake." Though such a line of thought sounds childishly irrational, some women find that it's all they need. It denies reality, including the reality that their unintended child is a human being. Sadly, these unplanned children become sacrificial victims to the thinking that someone *else* has to pay the price when things go wrong.

Isn't abortion justified for a woman whose other children are already grown?

Pregnancy sometimes presents a special fear for the older woman, because of the statistically higher risk that she will bear a defective child. Twenty-five percent of all Down's syndrome children, for instance, are born to women over thirty-five. But an older woman may simply fear or resent the demands a young child will place on her, particularly if she has already reared other children. Abortion, however, can't therefore be viewed as more "understandable" for the anxious older woman. Even if she thinks she has already paid her child-rearing dues, *this* child's right to life is as sacred as that of her other children. It must not be forfeited just because his mother is past a certain age.

Should a woman have to bear another child when she and her family can barely provide for their older children?

The case is sometimes made for abortion on the basis of financial necessity, when a family is already living in impoverished circumstances. "Another mouth to feed," the father sometimes groans. They question whether it is right to ignore the needs of the older children in order to make room for another child. Although such couples can consider placing a child for adoption if they cannot afford to care for him, this alternative almost always meets with negative attitudes, at least in the U.S. Aborting the child for financial reasons, however, does not disguise what abortion actually entails: as surely as any other, this abortion kills a child. The family may thereafter live in spiritual poverty if they take this course, especially if their financial condition later improves.

Isn't abortion needed as a means of controlling overpopulation?

The threat of overpopulation in the U.S., as in most Western nations, is a myth. The fertility rate in the U.S. has dropped to the point where society is more likely to suffer because of having too few people rather than too many — even with an immigration rate of about 400,000 per year.

A fertility rate of 2.1 per family is needed just to keep a population at a constant level. As the 1980s began, the U.S. had a rate of 1.8. Because more people are now living longer, the population's median age is rising, a fact that can easily lead to severe social and economic problems for the nation.

Factors that contribute to the falling fertility rate include the widespread use of birth control, the fact that many couples are electing to delay having children (if they have them at all), and the economic independence of women. Add to these reasons the frequent depiction of parenthood and family life as uncreative and unfulfilling, the increasing incidence of family breakdown, the diminishing influence of religion on personal morality, and the prevalence of divorce.

There is little reason to expect that the present trends in the U.S. population will be reversed in the near future. At the present pace, by 1995, the nation will have aborted 32 million babies since the Supreme Court decision of 1973. By 1995, there will be social and economic reasons—if no better ones—to miss these unborn children.

The Anatomy of Abortion

How many abortions have been performed in the U.S since 1973?

Since the U.S. Supreme Court decision of January 1973 that made abortion-on-demand the law of the land, there have been an estimated 10.2 million abortions in the U.S. through 1980. That estimate comes from the Alan Guttmacher Institute, the research arm of Planned Parenthood. Based on the rate of increase observed each year since 1973, an estimated 13.5 million abortions were performed in the U.S. as of the tenth anniversary of the Court's decision.

In 1980, almost a third of all pregnancies in this country ended in abortion, an unborn child being killed every twenty seconds. In 1978, abortions outnumbered live births in four-teen American cities.

Who are the women who obtain abortions?

In 1978, one third of all abortions done in the United States were performed on teenage girls. Another third involved women from ages twenty to twenty-four. Of pregnant girls fifteen and under, fifty-eight percent had abortions; as did forty-three percent of those from ages fifteen to nineteen. Seventy-five percent of the women who had abortions were unmarried. Although over two thirds of the abortions obtained in 1978 were performed on white women, the rate at which nonwhite women obtained abortions was 2.5 times greater in proportion to nonwhite women in the population.

Thirty percent of all abortions were performed on women who had had previous abortions.

Is the U.S. the only nation where abortion is legal?
Definitely not. About 38 percent of the people in the world live in a nation in which legal abortion is available on demand. Dreadful though its record is, the U.S. is not the world leader in incidence of abortions. That distinction would seem to belong to Russia. Using the latest available figures for each country, here are some comparisons: Russia, in 1970, had 700 abortions for every 1,000 pregnancies; Japan, in 1975, recorded 547 abortions per 1,000 pregnancies; Canada, in 1978, 148 per 1,000; West Germany, in 1979, 122; East Germany, in 1977, 260; France, in 1979, 170; and Sweden, in 1979, 264 per 1,000.

In 1980, in the United States, 300 abortions were performed for every 1,000 known pregnancies.

By what methods are abortions performed?
An abortion is usually performed by means of one or another of five techniques: suction (aspiration); dilatation and curettage (D & C); saline injection; prostaglandin injection; and hysterotomy.

Abortions done early in the pregnancy are normally accomplished either by the suction method or by means of a D & C. Abortions done during mid-pregnancy are usually done by saline injection or prostaglandin injection. Hysterotomy is reserved for abortions done late in the pregnancy—through the ninth month.

How is a suction (or aspiration) abortion performed?
A metal instrument is inserted into the vagina for the purpose of dilating (stretching open) the cervix, the opening to the womb. The cervix must be stretched to accommodate the abortion tools. One end of a metal or plastic tube is then in-

serted into the uterus, while the other end is attached to a powerful electric vacuum pump. The action of the pump tears the body of the unborn baby to pieces, then sucks those pieces through the tube and into a container.

How is a dilatation-and-curettage abortion performed?
The D & C requires that a metal instrument be inserted into the vagina to dilate the cervix. Then a curette, a loop-shaped steel knife, is inserted into the uterus. The abortionist cuts the unborn baby into pieces, which are then scraped out into a basin.

What is a D & E abortion?
A D & E, dilatation and evacuation, combines the abortion techniques of suction and D & C. D & Es are performed in the second trimester of pregnancy. Neither the aspiration (suction) nor the curettage method is used beyond the early weeks of the second trimester; so this method is utilized during the later weeks of the second trimester.

How is a saline-injection abortion performed?
A large, hollow needle is inserted through the woman's abdomen into the unborn baby's amniotic sac, and a concentrated salt solution is injected into the sac. The baby inhales and swallows this solution. Usually within an hour or two, the unborn baby goes into convulsions as a result of salt poisoning and dies. About a day later, contractions of the uterus begin and the mother gives birth to the baby, who is usually dead. The child's body exhibits severe burns from the salt solution. Occasionally the child is still alive and completes his death agony outside the womb. Some infants have survived this abortion technique and have been subsequently adopted.

How is a prostaglandin abortion done?

Prostaglandins are labor-inducing drugs. Such drugs have a legitimate use. But when labor and delivery are artificially induced well before the child is able to survive outside the womb, the result is the death of the premature child.

As in saline abortion, a hypodermic needle is inserted into the baby's amniotic sac through the mother's abdomen. The prostaglandin is injected, causing the uterus to contract intensely. Eight to twelve hours later, the baby—usually too small to have a chance for survival—is expelled from the womb as in childbirth.

How is a hysterotomy performed?

As with a delivery by Cesarean section, the mother's abdomen and uterus are surgically opened and the unborn baby is lifted out. This method is reserved for abortions done late in pregnancy, usually in the last trimester. Ordinarily, the baby is born alive but is left to die.

Do women really have third-trimester abortions?

Between one and two percent of all legal abortions done in the U.S. are late abortions, abortions performed after the unborn child is twenty weeks old and viable. About 90 percent of the nation's induced abortions take the life of the child during the first three months. Nonetheless, abortions in the last weeks and days of pregnancy are a reality.

Is a 'spontaneous abortion' or a D & C an abortion?

Spontaneous abortion is the technical term for a miscarriage. It is an act of nature. In ordinary speech, the word *abortion* refers to an *induced* abortion. One of the absurd scare tactics of the pro-abortionists is to say that if a human-life amendment to the Constitution is passed, women whose pregnancies end in miscarriage will be subject to prison terms.

The term D & C (dilatation and curettage) can also cause

confusion, since it is used to refer both to an abortive and a nonabortive procedure. A D & C *abortion* involves the deliberate killing of a child in the womb and removal of the remains. A physician will also use a D & C procedure to remove placental remains following a miscarriage, or to cleanse the womb of a uterine infection.

What other abortion methods are under development?
The Upjohn Company, of Kalamazoo, Michigan, which in the 1970s developed prostaglandin for use in abortion, is developing a do-it-yourself abortion kit for at-home use. Upjohn has been testing some of its products in countries where regulations are less demanding than those of the U.S. Food and Drug Administration.

A French physician-biochemist, Etienne-Emil Baulieu of the University of Paris, is developing a menstrual-regulation pill that may take the place of "the Pill." The French pill, RU-486, causes the onset of menstruation whether or not the woman is pregnant. It is claimed that this drug is better than the Pill because it puts fewer chemicals into the woman's body. It is taken on only four days of the monthly cycle rather than on twenty or twenty-one as the Pill requires.

The Upjohn kit and the French menstrual-regulation pill may, along with other scientific innovations, make abortion clinics "unnecessary" in the future. Biochemical killing in the privacy of one's own home will have become neater, cheaper, and disturbingly easy.

Where are abortions performed in the U.S.?
In 1980, abortions were performed at more than 2,750 hospitals and clinics across the U.S. Sixteen percent of those facilities (approximately 440) performed 75 percent of all the abortions done in the U.S in that year (about 1.2 million out of 1.6 million abortions), or about 2,800 per clinic.

How do abortion clinics function?

Most abortion clinics are privately owned, profit-making business enterprises. Some are sensitive about providing professional standards of care for the women who come to them. Others are not. Some provide a variety of "family-planning services," such as sterilization, while others do an abortion-only business.

Although the majority of abortion clinics seem to fulfill the requirements of the medical profession—by providing a pregnancy test, pelvic exam, counseling, medication, tissue analysis, birth-control pills, and a postoperative exam — others have treated their patients only a little less roughly than they have the unborn child.

There have been cases in which abortion procedures have been performed, in licensed clinics, on women who were not pregnant. Some of those women have suffered debilitating cramps, massive infections, and internal damage of such severity as to require the removal of all their reproductive organs. Incompetent and unqualified doctors, including moonlighting residents, have in some cases not waited for the painkilling anesthetics to take effect. In their moneymaking zeal, these doctors have sometimes done an abortion in two minutes instead of the ten minutes that medical authorities consider normal. "Counselors" in some clinics have been trained to sell the abortionists' services by means of sophisticated pitches and deceptive promises.

In spite of efforts by government agencies and outraged citizens to clean up these practices, abortion is destructive and violent in its very nature and leads to other sordid practices. As for the unborn child, whether the operation is done in a back alley or a gleaming modern hospital, suction tears, curettes cut, salt burns: abortion kills.

Does the unborn child suffer while being aborted?

Studies done by one specialist in fetal development, Dr. Albert Liley, reveal that a child may feel pain as early as the fifty-sixth day after conception. Special television cameras enabled him and other researchers to observe the spinal reflexes of the unborn child, which indicated sufficient development to feel pain.

By 120 days after conception, the nerves are developed sufficiently to allow the unborn baby to respond readily to pain and pressure. By the sixth month, the unborn's capacity to feel and react to pain is about equal to what it will be at birth.

Suction and curettage abortions both take about ten minutes. Pain is certainly felt as the procedures begin to tear the body apart, especially when done late in the first trimester and in the second trimester. The most painful method is the saline abortion. It takes from one to two hours for the salt solution to kill the unborn baby. Unlike the curettage or suction abortions, in which a random cutting or tearing of the body may quickly sever the baby's capacity to feel pain, salt poisoning, done in later stages of pregnancies, burns the baby's skin and his inner organs, no doubt producing acute pain for an extended period of time.

In the poignant words of a woman who had an abortion, the aborted baby's agony is reflected by "the agonized tautness of one forced to die too soon."

The Abortion Aftermath

What physical complications do women risk from early-term abortions?

Most abortions now done in the U.S. are done during the first three months of pregnancy. While the unborn's body is still relatively soft, the suction abortion and the dilatation-and-curettage (D & C) abortion are most commonly used. Both can result in frightening physical complications for the mother. These side effects range from the relatively minor, such as menstrual irregularity, to the potentially fatal, including hemorrhaging or blood-clotting.

In both of these early-pregnancy abortion procedures, the abortionist must first stretch open the cervix, or opening to the uterus. During the procedure, many women's bodies are injured—even before the abortion begins. Physicians say that the cervix normally is "green," or tightly closed, at this stage of pregnancy. This condition is one of nature's ways of protecting against miscarriage. Forcible stretching of the cervix can permanently weaken cervical muscles. Weakness of these muscles, in turn, increases the likelihood of later miscarriages and premature deliveries.

Women who have had two or more induced abortions are two to three times more likely than women who have never undergone an abortion to suffer miscarriages in subsequent pregnancies. Hemorrhage and infection are common after abortions by D & C or suction. Perforation of the wall of the uterus also occurs with unhappy frequency.

Abortion involves the separation of the blood-rich placenta (and the child) from the blood-rich uterus. Surgical knives and sharp-ended suction catheters are inserted by the abortionist, who must guess rather than see his way through the procedure. Failure to remove all fetal or placental tissue and surgical contamination cause infection in 25 to 35 percent of abortions. Perforation complications trouble women in 5 percent of the cases.

Urological complaints are also documented with increasing frequency in the medical literature. Subsequent pregnancies are often plagued by complications. Women who have had abortions are more apt to develop placenta previa, a condition in which the placenta covers the opening of the birth canal. This condition often necessitates delivery by Cesarean section.

What medical risks are involved in second-trimester abortions?

For the middle trimester of pregnancy (months four through six), salt poisoning (hypertonic saline instillation) is the "preferred method" to rid a mother of her baby. By this time, the baby is too big for the early-pregnancy solutions of scraping, cutting, or suctioning. But the saline abortion exposes the mother to some serious risks. The saline solution sometimes enters her bloodstream, subjecting her to risks of clotting, convulsions, coma, and cerebral damage.

Forcibly removing the child from his natural environment in the second trimester is three to four times more likely to result in maternal complications than if the abortion had been done in the first trimester. Women who undergo second-trimester abortions are more subject to infection, hemorrhage, and physical trauma.

Aren't abortions that are done late in pregnancy fairly safe?

The older unborn child is generally aborted by means of salt poisoning, hysterotomy, or prostaglandin injection. Both the salt and the prostaglandin injections cause violent labor contractions. The hysterotomy procedure is that of Cesarean-section delivery and is as "safe" as major surgery can be. Prostaglandin abortions have a 42 percent complication rate. In fact, all of these late abortions are quite dangerous for the mother because of the increased incidence of infections, hemorrhage, and cervical muscle damage.

What are the long-term physical troubles linked to abortion?
In addition to the increased incidence of subsequent miscarriage and premature delivery, abortion may permanently destroy a woman's ability to bear a child. Because infections and physical lacerations of the reproductive system are relatively common complications resulting from abortion, there may be scars in the fallopian tubes or in the uterus. Tubal scarring causes the chance of tubal (ectopic) pregnancy to jump from .5 to 3.9 percent, almost an 800 percent increase. Some women also have lengthy bouts with hepatitis, which they contract through blood transfusions. Transfusions are often necessary if hemorrhaging occurs following the procedure. Hepatitis can be fatal. Hemorrhaging itself can continue in some women and may eventually require surgery.

Do women who have abortions suffer psychological complications as a result?
Severe psychological complications can and often do haunt the woman who has chosen abortion. Studies have noted that psychic wounds can persist for decades. Pain, sorrow, and guilt are often somewhat delayed because the immediate post-abortion reaction is typically a feeling of numbnesss. Some women have ambivalent feelings about the abortion—experiencing relief and happiness at the same time as guilt and loss.

There is some evidence that teenagers who abort may be particularly prone to suicidal depressions. They sometimes attempt suicide on the date the baby would have been due.

Suicide is the fourth most frequent cause of death for teenage girls, and abortions among teens are relatively common.

A number of women who experienced anguish over their abortions formed a group called Women Exploited. They visit abortion clinics to talk with women about what abortion can cost them, physically and psychologically.

Do men experience distress over their aborted children?

Many men, even though they may have supported the abortion choice of the wife or girl friend, are burdened by feelings of guilt, hostility, and anger. The awareness that women can obtain abortions without their knowledge or permission causes some men to experience a sense of powerlessness. These fathers, studies show, are often untended mourners for their lost children, since it is women, not men, who are thought to need post-abortion counseling. And men are often guilt-laden when the women suffer physical or psychological complications as a result of an abortion.

Is psychological harm done to a woman's other children when she has an abortion?

Sociological research has documented that parental squabbling and violence in the home can damage a child terribly. What then might it do to a child to learn that an unborn sibling died by parental design? Would that sort of knowledge make a surviving child feel lucky? insecure? cheated out of a brother or sister? Would the surviving child wonder whether his parents had considered aborting him? Would that child wonder how much any life is worth? Would he begin to believe that, because parents give life to their children, they also have the right to take their lives if they wish to?

Do medical professionals experience distress about performing abortions?

Abortion bothers even those who believe in it and see a lot of it. A study of doctors who performed D & E abortions in the second trimester of pregnancy showed that even some of these abortionists were traumatized by the dilatation-and-evacuation procedure. This procedure requires that the fully-formed, unborn fetus be dismembered and removed, piece by piece, from the womb.

At hospitals in Cleveland, Grand Rapids, and Fort Lauderdale, nursing staffs have collectively refused to assist at abortions done past the midpoint of pregnancy. Some hospitals also unofficially admit that some staff members regularly performing late-term abortions complain of nightmares about fetuses, including dreams about live babies who survive the attempt to kill them. And in some hospital situations, medical personnel try to cope with the unsettling irony of treating women who are awaiting the birth of their babies, while preparing other women for abortions.

Has legalizing abortion eliminated the 'back alley' abortion?
Understandably, there are no reliable statistics available on the number of illegal abortions done each year. Only legal abortions become a matter of record. Patients and the pertinent circumstances of their abortions are reported to the state board of health. For various reasons, there are always some women who prefer to deal with the so-called back-alley abortionist, knowing that no record will be kept.

Nonetheless, the fact that the Hyde Amendment severely limits the amount of federal monies available for abortions has apparently not pushed many women toward the cheaper "back alley" abortions. A study done by the Federal Center for Disease Control in Atlanta (1981) found that only one percent of women who would have used federal funds to buy abortions opted for illegal abortion. In some states, up to 40 percent of the women who would have obtained abortions if federal subsidies had been available, had their babies instead. In other places, women who really wanted an abortion found the money somewhere to obtain one at a licensed facility.

Women obviously believe that legal facilities are safer; and they are—for them.

What happens when the child survives an abortion?
About four hundred babies each year initially "cheat" abortionist and mother by living through the abortion. All of these are late-pregnancy babies, most of whom were aborted by the saline-injection method. Most in fact do die soon after their surprising live exit from the womb. Salt poison has usually burned the skin all over the child's body. The child has often swallowed the saline solution, with the result that his internal organs are also damaged. A few infants have lived through this kind of trauma and were later adopted. But most often, the doctors order nursing staffs to ignore the live aborted child. In Omaha, for instance, in 1979, an aborted baby boy was left for two hours to die in a hospital utility closet. Abortionists fear legal complications when aborted babies fail to die in abortions. Most hospitals have no established procedures for dealing with this contingency. It is a "complication" they would rather not face. Some states have laws mandating that babies born alive during an abortion procedure be cared for, but such laws are practically unenforceable.

What happens to the baby's remains after the abortion?
The remains will usually be incinerated or trashed, especially in cases of early abortions. When the baby is aborted in the first trimester, body parts will literally be shredded by the D & C or by the suction process.

Body parts of babies aborted in late term are sometimes sold to commercial firms. In one case, the money was used by a hospital to buy furniture and to provide expenses for physicians attending conventions.

Sometimes the aborted babies are preserved so that they will later be available for research purposes. In February of 1982, the bodily remains of approximately 15,000 to 17,000 aborted babies were discovered in a large storage container that had been rented by a Los Angeles pathologist. Workmen had been sent to repossess the container. Inside they found small, plastic, formaldehyde-filled containers crammed with the bodies of babies who had been aborted at all stages of pregnancy. One workman commented, "They say they're just fetuses, but they sure looked like humans to me."

What might be the commercial use of all this "medical waste"? The answer may lie in the cosmetic industry's need for collagen, a gelatinous substance that can be extracted from the connective tissue, bone, and cartilage of these human remains. In early 1982, a Paris law journal reported that guards at the French border discovered a truckload of frozen human fetuses being shipped to cosmetic laboratories in France.

Is experimentation being done on the unborn child or the child who survives an abortion attempt?

Pharmaceutical companies have begun to take advantage of the guinea-pig potential of the unborn child who is scheduled for abortion. In May 1982, E. R. Squibb & Sons Company admitted that it was running tests on unborn children, with the cooperation of pregnant women who wanted to abort them. These women were injected with an experimental blood-pressure-control medication and then tested to assess the medication's value. Following the abortion, fetal blood samples and the placenta were examined.

In some far more gruesome research projects, rubella and other disease vaccines were injected into the womb and into the fetus to see what damage would result. Following the abortion of these infants, their infected bodies were dissected. Some infants who survived abortion attempts have been dissected alive for purposes of research. Researchers justify use of the living body of the unborn for experimentation on the grounds that the child is headed for abortion anyway. Besides, they reason, such research may lead to better prenatal care for unborn children who have the luck to be wanted.

Is abortion a big-dollar business?

Although costs vary regionally, authorities estimate that in the fall of 1980, a woman obtaining a first-trimester, complication-free abortion needed about $200. Based on the 1,647,134 legal abortions performed in 1980 (the number has increased every year since 1973), we can see that the total spent on this largely elective procedure is enormous. The gross proceeds are in excess of $320 million per year. Later abortions, costing as much as $1,000, boost the actual total. There are an estimated 30,000 of these each year in the U.S..

How does abortion affect our standard of living?

Legalized abortion, even apart from its moral implications, has an enormous impact on the standard of living in the U.S. And that effect will continue to grow in coming years. That's because abortion is one of the causes of a major fertility decline, in the U.S. and other "developed" countries. Soon, older segments of the population will constitute a much larger proportion, making it difficult for the younger, economically productive citizenry to keep up. The Social Security structure already seems to be collapsing because there are too few wage earners to support it.

In 1981-82, there were almost 5.5 million fewer children in U.S public primary and secondary schools than there had been ten years earlier. Private-school enrollment increased during that decade—but not by millions. The projection of continuing decline in the number of younger members of U.S. society is bad news for many industries. The customers won't be there for them to serve. And the children who will not grow up to become producers and consumers—and parents—will be recognized as a tremendous loss to the nation's basic economic resource.

Is society seriously affected by abortion?

Abortion and its kindred movements, euthanasia and infanticide, continue to take their toll in human lives. Exterminating fellow humans exacts a cost on society too. And that cost can never be counted. Killing those who inconvenience us is becoming an acceptable way of solving social problems. The interlocking social complex of trust that once marked personal relationships has been damaged. In a society that condones elective killing, parents kill children, children kill parents . . . all for "very good reasons."

One of the wise commentators on our time, Malcolm Muggeridge, put it this way: "In life-denying terms, as we have seen, compassion easily becomes a holocaust; garden suburbs and gulags derive from the same quest for quality of life, and the surgeon's knife can equally be used to sustain and extinguish life. Dostoevsky makes the same point: 'Love toward men, but love without belief in God, very naturally leads to the greatest coercion over men, and turns their lives completely into hell on earth.' " *(The Human Life Review,* Winter, 1980)

Women—Rights and Options

Isn't abortion just a woman's concern?
Abortion is too important an issue to be the domain of any group—even one as large as the world's entire female population. Because abortion is literally a human-life issue, it is the appropriate concern of every human being. The act of abortion itself takes the lives of unborn females and unborn males. Then too, the ravages and the costs of abortion touch both women and men.

Doesn't a woman have the right to control her own body?
This question sidesteps the issue. When a woman is pregnant, the biological fact is that there is another person growing within her. If "the right to control her body" is taken to include ending the life of an unborn child growing within her womb, then yes, she would have such a right. But to understand "her body" in that sense is both unscientific and illogical. A mother's natural obligation is to care for the welfare of her child; her body is so designed as to provide such care during the normal term of pregnancy. Do a mother's "rights" extend to a denial of what is natural to her?

If a woman doesn't believe in abortion herself, isn't it justifiable for her to be pro-choice for other women?
The self-described pro-choice woman may feel that there is something narrow-minded about not being pro-choice. The

current rhetoric may have encouraged her to see herself as backing, not abortion, but the freedom to choose to have an abortion. But what about the long-term consequences of this sort of "freedom"? Individuals who insist on having the "freedom" to fulfill their own desires soon become uncaring about the rights of others. Human lives fall victim to the "freedom" of the powerful individual to ignore the rights of others.

Freedom to choose abortion really means freedom to kill an unborn child. Maybe the one who chooses abortion would rather not pay attention to the abundant scientific evidence that shows the unborn to be a human person, but that reluctance doesn't change the reality. The child in the womb is a tiny human being on his or her way to birth, to life in the environment outside the womb.

The sad truth is that the present laws of the U.S., and of other nations, unfairly grant a license to kill by means of abortion. The number of tiny human victims each year is more than 1.5 million in the U.S. alone.

Aren't all feminists pro-abortion?

Feminism, as a theory, asserts the political, economic, and social equality of the sexes. And in practice, feminism is organized activity on behalf of women's rights and interests. Regardless of whether one speaks of the theory or the practice, feminism has nothing to do with abortion. In fact, a case can be made that to act on behalf of women's rights and to act in defense of abortion are mutually exclusive. After all, abortion makes women accomplices in the deaths of their children (and half of them are female children), an action that often haunts these women or harms them physically. One group that most emphatically takes this position is Feminists for Life (FFL). Started early in the 1970s, the group's members supported the Equal Rights Amendment and other feminist goals but vigorously opposed abortion. One member of FFL, Mary Ann Schaefer, has condemned the attempt to "marry" feminism to abortion as "terrorist feminism" because, as she put it, one then had to be "willing to kill for the cause you believe in. . . ."

Don't many men also feel that women should have the right to choose abortion?
Public opinion polls in the late 1970s and early 1980s have shown that only about one person in five believes that abortion on demand should be legal. A similar number of people feel that abortion should be illegal in all circumstances. Just about half of those polled approve of abortion for "hard" cases, such as when pregnancy is the result of rape or incest, or if the unborn child is diagnosed as handicapped.

A poll by the Associated Press and NBC News in August 1982 indicated that almost half of Americans—49 percent—believe that abortion is wrong; yet 62 percent of the poll's respondents said it should be legal, and that percentage included just over half of those who agree that it is wrong. Fifty-two percent of the women respondents said abortion is wrong, while 47 percent of the men said it is wrong.

It is significant that many people are still convinced that abortion is wrong even though it has been sanctioned by law in the U.S. since 1973.

Doesn't the growing number of women who have second and third abortions indicate that they find abortion a positive solution?
A study of those women who had sought a second, third, or fourth abortion in New York City in 1979 indicated that they made up almost 40 percent of aborting women there. Thus abortion was often a form of "backup birth control," a quick solution for women who wished to avoid the demands a child would place on them. Stress was found to be a common denominator among the women who opted for abortion. Most had experienced stressful situations within the previous year: death, a failed love affair, psychological or psychiatric counseling, a major gynecological problem, or an un-

stable life situation. An unwed 19-year-old explained that she had had her third abortion because she had been unable to find a suitable method of birth control. She insisted that she would never have a fourth abortion, saying, "I just can't keep on destroying babies."

Isn't abortion a medically safer choice for a woman than childbirth?
Abortion supporters have long insisted that undergoing an abortion is five to ten times safer than carrying a pregnancy to term. But that assertion is being effectively challenged. For one thing, it is hardly valid to compare mortality figures for women who've aborted in their third month of pregnancy with statistics for women who've gone the full nine-month term. (Childbirth mortality data also include deaths occurring as late as three months after delivery.)

Statistics can be deceptive in other ways too. Abortion-death statistics are arrived at by dividing the number of deaths among aborting women by the number of abortions. Maternal-death data, however, are incomplete to start with. All the maternal deaths from childbirth are divided only by pregnancies that result in live births. Left out are numerous cases of ectopic pregnancies and stillborn deliveries. Socio-economic comparisons between women who die during an abortion and women who die in childbirth should be considered. Women who give birth are more likely to be members of lower-income groups, for whom quality health care is less available.

When adequate research is available comparing the number of deaths of women during childbirth with deaths of women as a result of abortions, it may be found that abortion is the worse threat.

Don't women who have had abortions generally feel they have made the right choice?
In the years of fully legalized abortion in the U.S., there has

been less study of this aspect than one might expect. In 1975, a study was made of couples who had chosen abortion because tests indicated their child to be genetically handicapped. The study showed a higher rate of depression and regret among such parents than among those who chose abortion for other reasons. Some clinic questionnaires show that women who chose abortion experienced relief and happiness, having got rid of their "problem," but also a sense of grief and loss. On the other hand, some women show an amazing lack of insight into the meaning of abortion and seem almost uninterested in the life of the unborn inside them.

Won't women who have abortions be prosecuted for murder if a human-life amendment to the Constitution is passed?

The intention of a human-life amendment would be to give to the unborn the rights they enjoyed in most states before 1973, not to punish women who obtain abortions. Dr. John C. Willke, a pro-life educator and leader, was asked this question in late 1981. His reply was: "During the entire 200 years of our nation's history, and during a time abortion was outlawed and the unborn was protected from [the moment of] conception, abortionists were occasionally jailed. But there is not a single case in the record books of a woman being put in jail [for having an abortion]."

Wouldn't a human-life amendment put the value of the unborn's life above that of the mother?

Authorities in constitutional law insist that a human-life amendment would help to correct the glaring injustice by which unborn children are condemned to death without a hearing. The legal tradition of our nation once protected the unborn's right to live, to inherit, and to sue for damages. An amendment restoring the rights of the unborn would restore a balance upset by the Supreme Court, which legalized abortion-on-demand in 1973.

What alternatives to abortion are there for the woman with an unwanted pregnancy?

The initial alternative, of course, is to give birth to the child. If the woman chooses on behalf on the child's life, she then has some further alternatives. Her choice among these will most probably be made after careful consideration of her state in life, her age, her attitude toward the baby, and her family's attitudes toward the baby. She may choose to keep the child, or she may surrender the child for adoption. Even if the woman is married, giving the child up for adoption is a legal alternative if her husband agrees to it.

What help is available for women who want to keep their children, but for whom doing so would pose hardships?

A woman who chooses to keep her child will certainly need plenty of help in both the short and the long run. For an unmarried woman, the situation is most challenging. The sources of immediate help include some national-network pro-life agencies that help the mother to get reasonably priced health care throughout her pregnancy, supply expectant mothers with layettes, direct them to local or state assistance programs, and help them with requests for pastoral counseling. Birthright International and Alternatives to Abortion International are two such groups. In 1982, AAI had 1,100 chapters in the U.S., while Birthright had 500. Birthright's U.S. headquarters is in Woodbury, New Jersey. AAI maintains a national office in Toledo, Ohio. Local Right to Life groups can also be helpful. Many church agencies now offer assistance. Catholic diocesan programs offer a wide spectrum of services for women who wish to keep their babies. Programs are constantly being created in many localities to assist women whose pregnancies bring with them serious difficulties. In some communities, everything from layettes to emergency housing to psychiatric counseling is available.

What can a pregnant teenager do when she wants to have her baby but is pressured by parents to have an abortion?

A pregnant teen needs help in such difficult circumstances. Her best chance will be to make contact with a pro-life organization if there is one close by. Right to Life, Birthright, and Alternatives to Abortion International are often able to provide some immediate support. Even if she is a minor, a pregnant teen should know that her parents cannot legally force her to obtain an abortion.

What help is available for the woman who prefers to give her child up for adoption?

Though they have declined in number, fine maternity homes still exist to help a woman who has decided to give her child up for adoption. A telephone call or visit to local family-counseling agencies can help locate those homes. Other agencies, including diocesan Catholic social-service groups, can help the expectant mother to see that her baby will be placed with adoptive parents who are eager to have a child to love and care for. Because of the critical shortage of children available for adoption, an expectant mother will often have her pregnancy expenses paid through an adoption agency. In some areas of the country, there are ten waiting, childless couples for every adoptable child.

Is it 'natural' for a woman who has carried a child for nine months to give up the baby for adoption?

It is natural for a mother to want what is best for her child. An unmarried or very young mother may conclude that she simply cannot provide for her child. Though the pain of giving up a child may be with the woman for her lifetime, she may be consoled by the thought that the baby was given to a family who would love and provide for him or her. Just about 16,650 U.S.-born infants were placed in adoptive homes in 1980. According to the National Committee for Adoption, 1.5 million American couples want to adopt.

Birth Control and Abortion

What does the term 'birth control' really mean?
According to one current definition, *birth control* refers to control of the number of children born, especially by preventing, or lessening the frequency of, conception. Some, most notably the Planned Parenthood Association, insist that abortion should be classified as a method of birth control. Planned Parenthood also admits no difference between birth-control methods that prevent conception and so-called "birth controls" that kill unborn human life by preventing implantation in the womb (uterus) after conception has occurred. Others maintain that because abortion takes life once it has begun, it does not rightly belong in a category with birth controls that prevent but do not kill human life.

What are the various kinds of birth control?
By function, birth control can be divided into four types: barrier methods, nonbarrier methods, sterilization, and natural-family-planning methods.

Natural-family-planning methods are a special form of birth control because they can be used either to avoid or to accomplish conception.

Sterilization is sometimes challenged as a method of birth control because it goes beyond preventing conception at a given time. Sterilization eliminates fertility by rendering either the man or the woman sterile (permanently infertile).

How do barrier contraceptives work?

Barrier birth controls, or contraceptives, simply place a chemical or physical barrier between sperm and ovum to prevent fertilization. A few—for example, the condom—are used by the male, but most are used by the female.

The diaphragm is a barrier-type contraceptive used by women. Dome-shaped to fit over the cervix, it is often used in conjunction with chemical barriers, such as foams, jellies, and suppositories. The latter work to immobilize the sperm, which otherwise would naturally travel through the woman's cervical mucus toward the fallopian tubes, where fertilization normally takes place. When these chemicals act to kill the sperm, they are called spermicides.

The condom is a rubber or plastic casing worn over the penis during intercourse to prevent the release of sperm into the vagina.

How do the nonbarrier contraceptives work?

The nonbarrier methods alter or suspend the natural physiological functioning of the male or female reproductive system. A birth-control pill to be used by the male is being developed by pharmaceutical firms, but no such pill is yet available. Virtually all the contraceptives in this category are for use by the female. The two most common are the triple-function birth-control pill (or "the Pill") and the intrauterine device, or IUD. In fact, however, these products aren't properly included in a category with contraceptives, whose exclusive function is *preventing* conception. Occasionally the Pill kills newly generated human life. The IUD, on the other hand, consistently "controls" by killing unborn human life.

How does 'the Pill' occasionally abort newly conceived human life?

The most commonly used birth-control pill works in three ways: it inhibits ovulation (release of an ovum from an ovary); it stimulates the production of a type of mucus that frustrates sperm movement; and it makes the uterine lining temporarily incapable of sustaining and nourishing new human life.

The Pill introduces synthetic hormones—estrogen and progestogen (synthetic progesterone)—to the woman's body. There are different amounts of these hormones in different brands of pills, but all of these pills act to replace the estrogen and progesterone normally produced by the ovaries. They also thwart the hormonal message to the brain that triggers ovulation; ovulation is therefore suspended. Progestogen also stimulates the production of a type of cervical mucus that prevents the sperm from moving naturally through the uterus and into the fallopian tubes.

Occasionally, the Pill interrupts the normal growth of the lining of the womb. If ovulation and fertilization have occurred and if a new human life has reached the womb, it will be rejected, that is, aborted.

How does the IUD's abortive action work?

The IUD always "controls" by killing the new human life. Two of the three types contain either copper or a synthetic progestogen. All three varieties cause an inflammatory reaction in the uterine lining so that the new life is sloughed off and expelled. Medical science cannot wholly explain how the IUD accomplishes its goal; but it acts consistently as a silent abortifacient.

How does sterilization work?

In general, sterlization is the permanent impairing of a person's capacity to reproduce. Though attempts to reverse a sterilization procedure have had some degree of success, by and large, sterilization is a form of birth control that permanently closes the door to future children. Both men and women can be surgically sterilized. For a woman, sterilization is accomplished either by hysterectomy (removal of uterus and cervix), or, more often, by tubal ligation (cutting, or tying off, the fallopian tubes, through which the ova descend). Sterilization in men involves the tying off of the tubes through which sperm travel from the testes to the penis. This procedure is called a vasectomy.

How do natural-family-planning methods work?

Basically, natural-family-planning methods work by teaching couples to read the internal "clock" of the woman's cycle of fertility. By becoming sensitive to subtle changes in her physiology, a woman can tell when she is entering the brief period during which she can conceive in each menstrual cycle. If a couple do not wish to conceive, they must refrain from intercourse during this brief fertile period.

Changes in the cervix and cervical mucus are directly and hormonally linked to ovulation. As the time of ovulation approaches, the mucus becomes noticeably thin and elastic. The cervix itself softens, rises, and opens. The basal body temperature also rises soon after ovulation. Some NFP methods, such as the Billings Method, consider only the mucous symptoms. Others use only temperature as a fertility indicator. The Sympto-Thermal Method, as taught by the Couple-to-Couple League, uses the evidence of mucus, cervix, and temperature to determine the woman's fertile period.

Don't doctors explain that some birth-control methods are abortive?

Some may, but other medical authorities persist in blurring the distinctions. According to Dr. C. Everett Koop, the pro-life surgeon general of the Reagan administration, the American College of Obstetricians and Gynecologists has also openly advanced the cause of truth twisting. The ACOG has redefined *pregnancy* from "that period from conception to birth," to "that period from *implantation* to birth" in order to make the intrauterine device (IUD) more acceptable to American women. And many women who are "on the Pill" aren't informed that it too sometimes acts as an abortifacient.

Why be concerned that contraceptives cause early-pregnancy abortions, when nature often does the same thing?

Advocating the position implied by this question is like saying that because all people eventually die, it is all right to murder someone. It's true that natural factors often precipitate a spontaneous abortion, or miscarriage, of the very young conceptus. One study concluded that chromosomal abnormalities occur in possibly 10 percent or even 20 percent of pregnancies, thus causing unpreventable miscarriages. On the other hand, knowingly using a contraceptive that, at least at times, kills life in its tender beginnings is different. From that first moment of existence, beginning at conception, each human life should be respected.

All things considered, is there a 'best' method of artificial birth control?

Aside from the moral questions raised by some methods, the answer depends on what is meant by "best." The Pill, which frustrates the normal course of pregnancy, is near the top of the list of effective methods. But the Pill, along with the IUD, carries serious medical hazards along with its high effectiveness rating. Thrombosis (blood clots), heart attacks, strokes, high blood pressure, gall bladder disease, liver tumors, birth defects, subsequent pregnancy complications, and post-Pill infertility have all been statistically cited as side effects of the Pill. The Pill is also suspected as a cause of cancer of the cervix and uterine lining.

Use of the IUD increases risk of uterine or cervical perforation, infection in the pelvic area (a cause of abnormal bleeding, fallopian-tube disease, and ectopic pregnancy), menstrual disorders, cramps, and backache.

Though not likely to cause serious medical complications, the condom, withdrawal, and the diaphragm are less effective contraceptives.

Medical pioneering is now at work on brand-new birth-control methods. Skin implants of time-release contraceptives, effective for as long as a year, have been tested. One contraceptive, Depo-provera, is designed to be administered by injection at three-month intervals. It "controls" conception by altering the condition of the uterine lining, and thus acts essentially as an abortifacient. Medical problems haunt both of these new methods. In 1982, one organization, the National Woman's Health Network, announced it would lobby against government approval of Depo-provera (an Upjohn Company product) because of a link to cancer and birth defects.

Some experts testify that only natural-family-planning (NFP) methods score high on effectiveness, safety, and simplicity. With a 98-percent effectiveness rating, verified in numerous tests, NFP has the added moral edge over artificial methods for those individuals who reject artificial means of birth control. Not only do they have no problem with the natural methods, but they find them helpful as a legitimate method of child spacing.

Don't some opponents of abortion also oppose all contraception?

Pro-life people include both opponents and proponents of contraception, but they are of one mind about abortion: they oppose it. Some reject the use of contraception on moral grounds. Others are committed to the philosophical principle that people should not try to limit or eliminate procreation by unnatural means. But the two issues, abortion and contraception, though related, are fundamentally different. Abortion involves the deliberate ending of a human life, while contraception prevents a human life from beginning.

Why don't pro-life groups advocate contraception as 'the lesser of two evils'?

Pro-lifers know very well that many groups in our society already advocate the use of contraceptives, and that most women of childbearing age employ some form of birth control for a time during their fertile years. Contraception really doesn't "need" any more promoting in our society. What pro-lifers are doing is giving public witness against the destruction of innocent human life. There are more than a million and a half abortions annually in the U.S. alone. The prolife people say it shouldn't be necessary to deal with this moral and social problem of abortion by pushing an option —contraception—that is no better than "the lesser of two evils."

Wouldn't legislation outlawing abortion also make birth control illegal?
No. A human-life amendment to the Constitution, for example, would have no effect on the use or sale of birth-control pills or " morning-after" pills. Medical authorities are aware that these so-called contraceptives can, in fact, cause abortions during the first days of life. Sometimes, however, they genuinely act to prevent conception. No amendment or follow-up legislation would therefore attempt to prohibit them because they are not abortifacients in every case. It is possible, though not likely, that the IUD (intrauterine device) would be illegal, because its exclusive function is to expel the fertilized ovum from the womb.

Religion and Abortion

Does the Bible refer to abortion or to the unborn child?

The Old Testament makes just one reference to abortion, when it speaks of accidental abortion or miscarriage in Exodus 21:22-25. The Jews were instructed concerning liability for a pregnant slave who might be injured and miscarry while standing too near men fighting. The text demands that the responsible man compensate the woman's master. It adds that if she should die as a result, there should be a life-for-life reckoning.

A significantly different interpretation of this text appears in the Septuagint, the third-century Greek translation of the Old Testament. Here, the Exodus verse is said to demand a fine of the guilty party if the child is imperfectly formed (meaning a child in the early stages of pregnancy). If the child is perfectly formed (in the later stages of pregnancy), the responsible man "shall give life for life."

All through the Old Testament, however, the concept of human life as a God-given gift is present. One of the more beautiful references to the child in the womb occurs in Psalm 139:13-15. David, the Psalmist, praises God, saying, "It was you who created my inmost self, and put me together in my mother's womb; for all these mysteries I thank you: for the wonder of myself, for the wonder of your works."

In the Gospel according to Luke, the most dramatic reference to unborn life is made by Elizabeth, cousin of Mary, the mother of Jesus. "Blessed is the fruit of your womb," Elizabeth said, explaining that her own unborn child (who would become known as John the Baptist) had leapt for joy at the proximity of the unborn Christ.

But the New Testament does not make any explicit condemnation of abortion, though scholars suspect that St. Paul was doing just that in condemning the use of *"pharmakeia"* in his epistle to the Galatians. *Pharmakeia* was the practice of sorcery by means of drugs. Some of these drugs, it is thought, were abortifacients. In the New Testament as a whole there is a constant example of Christ-like defense of the weak, the sick, the little ones. And the entire ministry of Christ Himself says with every action and word that life is a gift from His heavenly Father, who is also ours.

What does the Catholic Church teach about abortion?

Since the time of the Apostles, in the first century, the Catholic Church has considered abortion an attack on a human life. Church Fathers often referred to the practice of abortion as "homicide" or "parricide"—the murder of a close relative. The Church still condemns abortion today as a violation of the commandment "Thou shalt not kill." *The Constitution on the Church in the Modern World*, produced by the Second Vatican Council, stated: "Therefore, from the moment of its conception, life must be guarded with the greatest care, while abortion and infanticide are unspeakable crimes." The popes have always condemned abortion as a great offense against the Creator of life.

In 1979, in Washington, D.C., Pope John Paul II said: "I do not hesitate to proclaim before you and before the world that all human life—from the moment of conception and through all subsequent stages—is sacred, because human life is created in the image and likeness of God . . . and when God gives life, it is forever."

Doesn't the Church permit abortion if the pregnancy threatens the woman's life?

The Church has never condoned the taking of innocent human life. The unborn child is and always has been regarded as an innocent human life. However, the Church does allow the death of the unborn child as an *indirect* result of therapeutic abortion under certain circumstances. An example is the case of an ectopic pregnancy, a pregnancy that develops in a fallopian tube instead of in the uterus. If left to develop in the tube, an ectopic pregnancy will rupture the tube and cause internal hemorrhage, possibly killing the mother. Catholic principles allow the surgical removal of the unborn child, which causes the young life to end. Such surgery does not *intend* the death of the unborn; that would be an indirect or secondary effect. The action's intent is to save the life of the mother. An unintended, but unavoidable, result is the death of the child.

Didn't St. Thomas Aquinas, a Doctor of the Church, believe that the unborn child is human only in the later stages of pregnancy?

St. Thomas believed that the unborn is human at every stage of pregnancy and taught that abortion is therefore always wrong. Dependent only upon the scientific knowledge of the thirteenth century, however, he did accept the ancient theory of delayed animation or ensoulment. This theory held that the unborn male became animated, or received a rational soul, around the fortieth day of uterine life, while the unborn female became animated at the ninetieth day. Evidence of the process of fetal growth was so primitive at this time that Aquinas's error is understandable. Thomas also believed that in the process of reproduction, the father's semen provided the only procreative material from which the new human life would grow. The mother, he theorized, provided only the nutrients and the fertile ground, so to speak.

Holding to this vision, Thomas and others of his day were forced to assume that the conception of Christ in the womb of the Blessed Virgin was an exception to this rule. Otherwise, Christ too would not have received an immortal rational soul, or animation, until His fortieth day—a reality that theologians knew to be inconsistent with biblical teaching that Christ was fully God and fully man from the first moment of Incarnation.

In fact, Church teaching updated the Aquinas theory about ensoulment or animation long ago. Now Church instruction maintains that animation and conception (or fertilization) happen at the same moment. In other words, the unborn is completely human from the beginning.

Hasn't the Church permitted abortion in the past?

From the very first decades of Christianity, the Church's condemnation of abortion has been clear and consistent. The *Didache* (or *The Teaching of the Twelve Apostles*) was most probably written before the end of the first century and served to instruct Christians. Some of the Fathers of the Church later valued the *Didache* as the most important source of Christian teaching next to the Bible. In a section titled "The Way of Life," the *Didache* cautions Christians against abortion and infanticide. "You shall not kill the fetus by abortion, or destroy the infant already born," it says. In fact, such practices were quite common in the cultures surrounding the newly blossoming Christian communities. The unbending prohibition against abortion and euthanasia by Christian authorities was often pointed to as one of the differences between pagan and Christian beliefs.

Doesn't the Church's opposition to abortion result from its opposition to artificial birth control?

The Church opposes abortion because it teaches that human life begins at the moment of conception. Since this is the case, the Church forbids abortion for the same reason that it forbids murder: both actions take an innocent human life, which the Church believes is sacred by its very nature.

The Church teaches that artificial birth control, a twentieth-century innovation, is wrong for a different reason. In his 1968 encyclical *Humanae Vitae* (Of Human Life), Pope

Paul VI built upon the historic teachings of the Church. Among the teachings was the statement from the Second Vatican Council's document *Gaudium et Spes* about the nature of marriage. "Marriage and conjugal love are by their nature ordained toward the begetting and educating of children," the Council stated. Paul VI, carrying this idea further, said that any act that separates the unitive and procreative aspects of conjugal love is wrong. They are naturally intended to work together, the Pope said, and the procreative power should not be unnaturally frustrated.

Do other religious groups oppose abortion?

Many churches and religious groups oppose abortion because they maintain that human life is a God-given gift. On record in opposition to abortion are various Eastern Orthodox Churches, the Lutheran Church (Missouri Synod), many congregations of the Church of Christ, the Church of Jesus Christ of the Latter-Day Saints (Mormons), the American Baptist Association, the Baptist Bible Fellowship, Orthodox Jews, and the National Association of Evangelicals. Three of the four largest Black Protestant denominations have also issued strong pro-life statements. In addition, three of the world's major religions—Islam, Buddhism, and Hinduism—are opposed to abortion.

Has there been any organized ecumenical opposition to abortion?

In 1982, a statement opposing abortion and related trends in the U.S. was signed by two hundred religious leaders and thinkers. Among the signers were: Roman Catholics, Father Theodore Hesburgh and Dr. Michael Novak; Protestants, Dr. John Warwick Montgomery, Dr. Francis A. Schaeffer, Dr. Harold O. J. Brown, Dr. Paul Ramsey; and Jews, Rabbi Seymour Siegal and Rabbi David Novak. The manifesto was prepared by the Christian Action Council and edited by Evangelical theologian Carl Henry. The statement:

We affirm that all human life is sacred because each human being bears the image of God. We oppose the devaluation of human life manifested in the widespread practice of abortion in America and the world, and in the growing tendency of some to value human life only if they deem it meaningful. We affirm the sanctity of each human life regardless of intelligence level, physical appearance, stage of development, or degree of dependency. We deny that any man or woman possesses the authority to judge some human beings as unworthy of life. We recognize that the Judeo-Christian ethic especially responds to the needs of the weak and unwanted. We encourage all efforts to help women facing unwanted pregnancies, to aid children and others suffering physical or mental handicaps, and to protect all human life under the law.

Aren't the religious groups that are trying to stop abortion forcing their morality on others?

Religious groups that are trying to bring a halt to abortion are attempting to bring their religious principles to bear in a society that allows religious freedom, and on that society's public laws. But these groups don't *force* their "morality" on anyone. They lobby on behalf of social attitudes that involve respect for life; and they publicize the principles they support. Such activity lies within the legitimate scope of freedom of speech and freedom of religious expression—guaranteed by the First Amendment. If they were to abuse the electoral processes, or attempt to bribe lawmakers, or monopolize public media, then one might say that they were "forcing their morality" on others.

Isn't when human life begins a religious question?

It is a scientific question, for which the answer can be demonstrated by observing the facts. It is a biological fact that at the moment of conception, the new life is neither vegetable nor animal; the new life is demonstrably *human.* Common sense also certifies that the being conceived by sexual union of a man and a woman is a human being, and that human life begins at the beginning.

A Christian or Jew will believe that a human life from the moment of conception is made in the "image and likeness" of God and possesses a soul; and that each human being is part of God's family and is a gift from God. These beliefs do not deal with when human life begins but with its relationship to its Creator, with what it is and, by extension, what its purpose may be.

Some who reject the statement that human life begins at conception are either unaware of, or willing to deny, that which is scientifically demonstrable. Others have arbitrarily picked a starting point for humanness—viability, birth, three days after birth, two years after birth—that fits their social or political agenda. For these people, the real question is not when human life begins but at what point human life is worth preserving. The answer to the question "When does human life begin?" has profound moral and religious implications.

Doesn't the involvement of churches in the abortion controversy violate the principle of 'separation of Church and State'?

In dealing with religious freedom, the First Amendment to the U.S. Constitution says that "Congress shall make no law respecting an establishment of religion, or prohibiting the free exercise thereof." This amendment is sometimes held up by separationists as proof that church groups that take public stands on abortion are acting unconstitutionally. They say the view that human life begins at conception is a religious belief only.

What separationists really want is to separate law from traditional Judeo-Christian morality. They would endorse this statement: "I personally oppose abortion but support the right of others to have abortions." This exaggerated notion of separation of Church and State also ignores the fact that before the early 1970s, Church and State both actively defended unborn life. Legal rights of the unborn were upheld at every level of the judiciary.

But separationists don't wish to detach law from all notions of morality. While some accuse pro-life individuals and groups of attempting to impose their religious convictions on society, separationists commonly defend with religious and moralistic fervor a woman's right to "control her own body," and perhaps also the right of a poor woman to have her abortion paid for out of tax monies. Moral arguments are supplied in abundance to defend a woman's "right" to be rid of an unwanted child, even to the point of suggesting that such a solution would also be "the right thing" for the child.

Who then may form public policy? Only those who lack Judeo-Christian moral convictions? Only those who are willing to abandon their Judeo-Christian moral convictions when it comes to public policies?

Do some atheists and agnostics oppose abortion?

Some atheists and agnostics have joined with believers in publicly opposing abortion. One of the most telling statements, made by an atheist who changed his thinking about abortion, is that of Dr. Bernard Nathanson, a founding father of the National Association for the Repeal of Abortion Laws (NARAL), which was later renamed the National Abortion Rights Action League. He had formerly served as the director of the largest and busiest abortion clinic in New York.

I think that abortion policy ought not be beholden to a sectarian creed, but that obviously the law can and does encompass moral convictions shared by a variety of religious interests. In the case of abortion, however, we can and must decide on the biological evidence and on fundamental humanitarian grounds without resorting to scriptures, revelations, creeds, hierarchical decrees, or belief in God. Even if God does not exist, the fetus does.—Aborting America *(1979).*

For Nathanson and many others who come to the defense of the unborn for nonreligious reasons, their action is based on the inescapable biological fact that human life exists from the moment of conception.

Are the religious groups that oppose abortion also opposed to euthanasia?
Some Protestant churches and Orthodox Jewish bodies have been quite outspoken in their objections to euthanasia. They have condemned it as an assault on the sanctity of human life and the religious conviction that the decision to end a human life belongs to God alone.

The Catholic Church has also repeatedly confronted the movements that favor mercy-killing, the legalization of suicide, "the right to die," and infanticide. In its *Declaration on Euthanasia* (1980), the Church presented guidelines for clergy and laity, who are both increasingly faced with questions about the prolongation of life. Rejected was any action leading to "the killing of an innocent human being." But the declaration also pointed out that when death is inevitably close, one is permitted in conscience to refuse forms of treatment that would only secure "a precarious or burdensome prolongation of life." The Catholic Church did insist that "the normal care due to a sick person in similar cases not be interrupted."

The declaration reaffirmed that "no one is permitted to ask for this act of killing; . . . nor can he or she consent to it." That ruled out the "right to die" asked for by some for people with terminal illness. The role of conscience—that of the patient, that of his doctor, and that of any person who may speak for the patient—was upheld. Here, conscience is said to be properly involved in deciding treatment, short of decisions to kill directly or to withhold ordinary treatment.

Abortion and the Law

When was abortion legalized in the U.S.?
Abortion on demand was uniformly legalized for all states of the United States by the Supreme Court decision of January 22, 1973.

How did the movement to make abortion completely legal begin?
The first state to prohibit abortion by statute was Connecticut, in 1821. By 1900, almost every other state had passed laws prohibiting abortion except when the mother's life was at stake.

The movement to legalize abortion beyond the rather specific restrictions of the law began in earnest in 1962. In that year, the American Law Institute proposed in its "Model Penal Code" that abortion should be legalized in the following circumstances: (1) when a pregnancy might harm the health of the mother, (2) when pregnancy is the result of rape or incest, and (3) if the pregnancy is likely to result in the birth of a child with severe abnormalities. These circumstances were called "hard cases," and abortions in those cases were referred to as "therapeutic."

Colorado, in 1967, was the first state to adopt liberal conditions for abortion. New York, in 1970, adopted the most liberal abortion law of all—making abortion legal in that state for *any reason* during the first 24 weeks of pregnancy.

By 1971, controversy over the growing liberalization of

abortion statutes had become intense. Although thirteen states had by then liberalized their abortion laws, more than thirty others had refused to do so.

The Supreme Court began hearing arguments on the abortion question in 1971 and continued to do so in 1972. On January 22, 1973, the Court announced its fateful decision in *Roe v. Wade* and *Doe v. Bolton*.

Didn't the Supreme Court legalize abortion only in the first three months of pregnancy?
No; it legalized abortion for all nine months of pregnancy. It did treat each of the three trimesters of pregnancy somewhat differently.

Is abortion absolutely legal during the first trimester (three months) of pregnancy?
Concerning the first three months of pregnancy, the Court said, "For the stage prior to approximately the end of the first trimester, the abortion decision and its effectuation must be left to the medical judgment of the pregnant woman's attending physician."

The Court allowed almost no restriction on abortions in the first trimester. It did grant states the power to require that abortions be performed by licensed physicians.

How about the second trimester? Is abortion completely legal then?
In theory, no; in practice, yes. Concerning months four through six of pregnancy, the U.S. Supreme Court declared: "For the stage subsequent to approximately the end of the first trimester, the State, in promoting its interest in the health of the mother, may, if it chooses, regulate the abortion procedure in ways that are reasonably related to maternal health."

This meant that a state may regulate the circumstances in

which abortions are performed—the facilities and the medical procedures, for example—but it may not prohibit them. In fact, however, most restrictions legislated by individual states have since been declared unconstitutional.

Abortion isn't legal during the third trimester, is it?
Yes—with some qualifications. This aspect of the Supreme Court's decision is the one most persistently misunderstood. Many people still don't realize that the Court legalized abortion, virtually on demand, at any time during the entire nine months of pregnancy.

Concerning the final three months of pregnancy, the Court said, "For the stage subsequent to viability, the State in promoting its interest in the potentiality of human life may, if it chooses, regulate and even proscribe abortion except where it is necessary, in appropriate medical judgment, for the preservation of the life or health of the mother."

What is "appropriate medical judgment"? Simply the advice of a doctor. What does "health of the mother" include? In reality, virtually anything—preservation from stress, inconvenience, annoyance, anything that upsets her sense of well-being.

What reasons did the Court give for legalizing abortion?
The Court cited the right of privacy, protected by the due-process clause of the Fourteenth Amendment, which the Court decided included a woman's decision about whether or not to have an abortion. The Court also decided that the word *person*, as used in the Fourteenth Amendment, did not include the unborn.

Didn't the Court's decision leave the matter of when human life begins an open question?
The Court recognized that opinions vary as to when human life begins but declined to offer its own opinion on the mat-

ter. The Court did say that the fetus becomes viable (able to survive outside the womb) between 24 and 28 weeks after fertilization. That would seem to imply that the Court accepted the fetus as a human life, beginning at 24 to 28 weeks but not before. So why did the Court legalize abortion beyond 28 weeks? In fact, the Court recognized a right to abortion whether the unborn was human or not.

Can a state legislate at all concerning abortion?

Yes and no. The Supreme Court said that a state may legislate as long as its laws "reasonably relate to the preservation and protection of maternal health," but only after the first trimester of pregnancy.

Regulations permitted to the states include determining qualifications of doctors performing abortions, setting standards for facilities in which abortions are performed, and the licensing of doctors and facilities.

The individual state may do these things, but that doesn't mean that the state laws would be upheld by the Court. Many states have prohibited certain methods of abortion—saline abortion, for example. Some have passed legislation to attempt to prevent suffering by the fetus. None of these statutes has been upheld by the Court. It seems that the Court is reluctant even to permit the states to make abortion less agonizing for the tiny victim.

Can't states pass laws to protect the baby who survives an abortion attempt?

According to the Supreme Court, the state may regulate abortion during the third trimester except in cases in which the mother's life or health is endangered. But it certainly hasn't worked out that way.

Two highly publicized cases illustrate that sad reality. In 1976, Kenneth Edelin, a Massachusetts physician, was accused and convicted of manslaughter after cutting off oxygen from a 21- to 24-week-old unborn child who was alive after a hysterotomy. Edelin's conviction was reversed by the Massachusetts Supreme Court. In a similar case, William Waddill, a California doctor, was charged with strangling a 31-week-old unborn child who survived a saline abortion. Waddill's case was dismissed after two trials resulted in hung juries. Although the babies were viable, they were nonetheless deprived of life.

In *Colautti v. Franklin* (1979), the Supreme Court struck down a Pennsylvania law stipulating that full professional care must be given to any baby who was viable when aborted. The Court also said that the doctor must select an abortion procedure that would be least painful to the baby. The Court said that the doctor could not be held liable for the death of the fetus and that the matter of viability should be left completely to the judgment of the doctor. Thus, the Court practically stripped the state of any real regulatory powers—and the child of any legal protection for his life.

Does the father of an unborn child have the legal right to participate in the abortion decision?
No. The Supreme Court, in *Planned Parenthood v. Danforth* (1976), invalidated a Missouri law that required written spousal consent before a married woman could obtain an abortion.

The Court reasoned that since it is the woman who is pregnant, she should be entitled to make the decision with regard to an abortion. No consideration was given to the role of the husband in creating the new life or to his interest in the unborn child. The spousal-consent law was seen as violating the woman's right to make a free choice.

In 1973, the Supreme Court said that a woman is free to have an abortion without the interference of the state. In 1976, the Court declared that a woman is free to have an abortion without the interference of her husband. The Court argued that the requirement of spousal consent would be damaging to the marriage relationship. No consideration was given to the possible damage to the marriage relationship that might result from lack of agreement on this crucial issue.

Don't parents of an unmarried minor have the legal right to prevent her from having an abortion?

No. In *Planned Parenthood v. Danforth* (1976), the Supreme Court invalidated both spousal consent and parental consent for an unmarried minor seeking an abortion. The unconstitutionality of parental consent was further established, in 1979, in *Bellotti v. Baird*. The rationale offered against spousal consent (see the preceding section) was offered here too.

It has gone differently with regard to parental notification. The Supreme Court upheld, in *H. L. v. Matheson* (1981), a Utah law requiring a doctor to notify the parents of an unmarried minor seeking an abortion. The reasoning was that mere notification doesn't take away her right to an abortion. Notification laws do not give parents the legal right to prevent their unmarried minor child from having an abortion.

What is 'informed consent'?

The purpose of an informed-consent law is to assure that the woman planning an abortion knows the facts about abortion and fetal development, and that her choice is freely made.

Informed consent may involve no more than a woman's certifying in writing that she is informed and that she has freely given consent to the abortion. Many states have legislated this type of informed consent. In some states, informed-consent legislation requires that a licensed physician explain to the woman the abortion procedure to be used, possible consequences to her health, alternatives to abortion, and the facts of fetal development. Many states have also legislated a 24- or 48-hour waiting period between the time the information is given and the time scheduled for the abortion.

Is 'informed consent' legal?

By early 1983, the Supreme Court had not issued a definitive ruling on the constitutionality of informed-consent laws, though the matter was pending. Lower court rulings have been inconsistent and contradictory. In *Planned Parenthood v. Danforth*, the Supreme Court upheld general informed-consent provisions, and, in *Planned Parenthood Association v. Fitzpatrick* (1976), the Court upheld more specific provisions. Yet, in *Planned Parenthood League v. Bellotti* (1981), a court of appeals struck down the provision requiring a doctor to provide information on fetal development. The 24-hour waiting period was also ruled unconstitutional.

Don't informed-consent provisions cause unnecessary stress for the woman planning to have an abortion?

The decision to destroy an innocent human life, however rationalized, is stressful. If, before the abortion, the woman is not aware of alternatives to abortion, possible medical complications, and relevant facts of fetal development, she will likely become aware of them sometime after the abortion. Then the guilt, anxiety, and remorse of the mother may even be irreparable.

Are abortions funded by the federal government?

Not since the passage of the first Hyde Amendment in 1976 have substantial federal funds been used to pay for abortions. The Hyde Amendment, named for its sponsor, Congressman Henry J. Hyde of Illinois, has been reenacted each new fiscal year. It is attached to the annual appropriations bill that provides funds for the Department of Health and Human Services (formerly Health, Education and Welfare). This is the department that administers the funding of abortion through the Medicaid program.

Each year since 1976, the Hyde Amendment has permitted some limited funding of abortion "to preserve the life of the mother." In some years, it included some funding for abortion of pregnancies resulting from rape or incest, and in cases where pregnancy could seriously harm the mother's health.

The Supreme Court upheld the Hyde Amendment, in *Harris v. McRae* and *Williams v. Zbaraz* (1980), ruling that it did not impinge "on the constitutionally protected freedom of choice recognized in *Wade*."

Why does federal funding for abortions continue to be a hot issue?

Abortion is a big business, and where public money is involved, the business usually gets bigger.

In 1980, it was estimated by Secretary of Health and Human Services Patricia Harris that without the Hyde Amendment the government would have paid for 470,000 abortions. The cost: $88 million! Under the Hyde Amendment, the estimated number of abortions to be publicly funded was 2,000—95.5 percent fewer.

Are hospitals, physicians, and other medical personnel required by law to participate in abortions?

Most states provide for some type of individual-conscience clause. This provision releases private, but not necessarily public, hospitals and their employees from performing or participating in abortions if doing so would be contrary to conscience. Individual-conscience laws have not yet been found unconstitutional. The courts, however, are not likely to tolerate state laws that would make abortion virtually unavailable as long as the Supreme Court decision of 1973 is the standard of constitutionality.

Was the Supreme Court decision legalizing abortion an abuse of its authority?

Justice Byron White, writing for the minority in the 1973 Supreme Court decision, called the ruling "an exercise of raw judicial power . . . an improvident and extravagant exercise of the power of judicial review that the Constitution extends to this Court."

The Tenth Amendment to the Constitution states: "The powers not delegated to the United States by the Constitution, nor prohibited by it to the States, are reserved to the States respectively, or to the people." There is nothing in the Constitution that guarantees the right to abortion, so it follows that the Court legislated the right. Many constitutional experts, including some who are pro-abortion, have been critical of the logic of the Court's decision.

Shouldn't abortion remain legal in the U.S. until the reasons for it are eliminated?

The most frequently cited "reason" for a woman's seeking an abortion is that she simply doesn't want the child. The real reason is a growing disrespect for life in the U.S. and a weakening of the support-system for minors and adult women who are searching for help or direction. The legalization of abortion has only served to encourage that disrespect for life and further weaken the support-system by encouraging women to think that abortion is the only help they need.

In any society, whatever is legal tends to become acceptable. The fact that abortion is legal acts as a positive encouragement to kill unborn children. But to legalize an act doesn't make that act moral. A society cannot long permit an immoral act to remain legal before the members of that society begin to lose respect for the law in general.

What can be done to overturn the Supreme Court's decision legalizing abortion?

There are three possible ways to overturn the present permissive abortion laws: judicial reversal, legislative action, or a constitutional amendment. A judicial reversal would require the Supreme Court to overrule its own 1973 ruling. Although the membership of the Court changes, judicial reversal is really very unlikely. That would involve not only setting aside the 1973 ruling but overturning many later rulings made in consequence of the original ruling.

Some legislative action is a prospect, but state legislatures and Congress cannot overturn a Supreme Court interpretation of the Constitution. Both can attempt to make laws that minimize a Court decision. Congress also has the power to make findings of fact (such as an answer to the question *When does human life begin?*) that could influence future judicial decisions. Congress may also attempt to regulate the jurisdiction of federal courts with regard to abortion issues.

Amending the Constitution is generally considered the best means of overturning the Supreme Court's decision. Still, that isn't easy either. Those who want a constitutional amendment disagree on what type of amendment is best. Once one is proposed, it must be passed by two thirds of both houses of Congress. Once that is achieved, three fourths of the states must ratify the amendment before it becomes part of the Constitution. The procedure is long and difficult, but it is probably the best chance available for the unborn in the U.S.

What chance would Congress have of overturning the Supreme Court's abortion decision of 1973?
If Congress tried to overturn the Court's decision through legislation, the Court would not uphold such legislation. In the 1982 session, a human-life bill was introduced in Congress. Its purpose was to establish, first, "significant likelihood that actual human life exists from conception"; second, that the intention of the Fourteenth Amendment is "to protect all human beings"; and, third, that *person* includes all human beings.

The first assertion involves a matter of biological fact and is generally considered to be acceptable to the Court. The second assertion might also be accepted. Most constitutional experts doubt that the Court would uphold the third provision, which contradicts the Court's 1973 assertion that the unborn are not persons in the sense in which the Constitution speaks of persons.

Such a bill, even if ruled unconstitutional, might be the

first step toward the establishment of laws that assure the unborn of their fundamental right to life.

How would a constitutional amendment protect the unborn?

The Helms-Lukens Amendment (proposed in 1982) spells out the protective measures and the "teeth" needed to make the amendment work should such an amendment someday pass.

Section 1 reads: "The right to life is the paramount and most fundamental right of a person." This section would establish the priority of the right to life over the "right" to abortion.

Section 2 reads: "With respect to the right to life guaranteed to persons by the fifth and fourteenth articles of amendments to the Constitution, the word 'person' applies to all human beings, irrespective of age, health, function, or condition of dependency, including their unborn offspring at every stage of their biological development, including fertilization."

Section 3 reads: "No unborn person shall be deprived of life by any person: provided, however, that nothing in this article shall prohibit a law allowing justification to be shown for only those medical procedures required to prevent the death of either the pregnant woman or her unborn offspring, as long as such law requires every reasonable effort be made to preserve the life of each." This provision would prohibit abortion except for the purpose of saving the life of the mother.

Section 4 reads: "Congress and the several States shall have power to enforce this article by appropriate legislation." This last section is needed because, though a constitutional amendment can recognize the right to life of the unborn, it takes legislation to enforce it.

Is there any other kind of amendment that would protect the unborn?

Another variety that has been proposed is a federalism

amendment, somewhat mistakenly identified as a states'-rights amendment. An example is the Hatch Amendment, proposed in the 1982 Congress. It reads: "A right to abortion is not secured by this Constitution. The Congress and the several States shall have the concurrent power to restrict and prohibit abortion."

This proposal returns power to the states to restrict abortion. It gives Congress as well the power to restrict and prohibit abortions. This sort of approach seeks to avoid the creation of legal-on-demand "abortion havens." It would authorize the lawmaking power of both the states and Congress, and allow the toughest hold on abortion to prevail in cases where they conflict.

Euthanasia

What does the term 'euthanasia' mean?
The term *euthanasia* is derived from the Greek *euthanatos*
and literally means "good death." It has two basic forms:
mercy killing and death selection. As the term is most commonly used today, it refers to mercy killing. Further distinctions are made between *active* and *passive* euthanasia, and
voluntary and *involuntary* euthanasia.

Mercy killing is the intentional use of medical procedures
or the denial of ordinary, needed procedures—either of which
will induce or hasten death. By definition, supporters of euthanasia are motivated by the belief that death is the merciful
answer for a sick or suffering person.

Active euthanasia, also called positive euthanasia, is the
deliberate taking of the life of a person suffering from an in-
curable condition or disease, whether by administering a
lethal drug or by withholding ordinary medical care.

Passive, or negative, euthanasia is the discontinuation of
an *extraordinary* life-preserving means. Many moralists do
not regard this as a form of mercy killing. But because the
question of what is "ordinary" and what is "extraordinary"
medical care or treatment is disputed, the distinction between
active and passive euthanasia is not always easy to make.

Voluntary euthanasia is either self-administered or administered by another person with the patient's consent. It's a
form of suicide. Involuntary euthanasia is administered by
another person without the patient's consent. It is a form of
homicide.

Shouldn't a person with a painful terminal illness have a right to take his own life?

Some proponents of euthanasia say the person should have that right. They want legalization of "voluntary euthanasia," which means legalization of suicide. Suicide is illegal in the U.S., and is objectionable on religious and ethical grounds.

But the movement to make euthanasia acceptable is gaining momentum. In 1980, England's Society for the Right to Die with Dignity (also known as Exit) published a do-it-yourself handbook on suicide, *A Guide to Self-Deliverance.* In 1982, *Suicide: Mode D'Emploi* (Suicide: Operating Instructions) became a bestseller in France. An English translation of the book is to be published. A popular play entitled *Whose Life Is It Anyway?* (1980) portrayed suicide sympathetically.

Some advocates of euthanasia in the U.S. seek to have suicide established as a constitutional right. Establishment of such a "right" would clear the path for recognition of a "right to assist" even the incompetent adult or the infant to commit suicide. A theory of "substituted judgment" is based on the assumption that the individual would have wanted to commit suicide, thereby making it permissible for another to "commit suicide for" him or her under constitutional protection.

A law permitting some persons to perform the act of suicide on other persons—so to speak—would provide a neat rationalization for getting rid of "undesirables" in several categories, including handicapped or retarded children. It would open the door for *involuntary* euthanasia, now still regarded as a form of murder. The distinction between "assisted suicide" and murder might easily become blurred. But perhaps the most tragic result of creating a so-called right to suicide would be that it would encourage people to escape from their problems rather than solve them.

In France, suicide victims have been discovered clutching their how-to-do-it manual. The book is likely to have similar results in the U.S. and elsewhere.

What is 'death selection'?

Death selection, also known by the elegant-sounding euphemism *managerial euthanasia*, is the decision to terminate lives judged to be no longer useful. The "unuseful" might be the bedridden grandmother, the senile gentleman, the retarded man, the paralytic. As in mercy killing, the person's life is intentionally taken. Proponents of death selection suggest that the life-or-death decision be made by a committee of hospital or community "professionals." The value of a person is measured only in terms of what he or she can produce. There is no acknowledgment of the inherent dignity of the human person. Rather there is an obsession with controlling the "productivity profile" of the human race.

Is euthanasia legal in the U.S.?

No, it is not. In U.S. law, euthanasia is considered homicide, regardless of the motive. It is also sometimes a difficult charge to prove. Yet, even when evidence would seem sufficent, sentiment in favor of euthanasia is surfacing in court decisions. Early in 1982, in a much-publicized case of mercy killing, 69-year-old Woodrow Collumns, of San Antonio, Texas, was found guilty of killing his older brother, who was terminally ill. On November 16, 1981, Collumns went to the hospital room of his brother, a victim of Alzheimer's disease, and shot him six times. Collumns was placed on ten-years probation and required to work ten hours a week at a nursing home. His crime could have netted him life in prison if it had been dealt with as a homicide.

Is euthanasia practiced in the U.S.?

Certainly. Just how often is impossible to say, but it is fairly clear that the most common targets are the elderly, the retarded, and the handicapped newborn. They are the least able to defend their rights and the most likely to be seen as a drag on the rest of "productive society." The medical literature of recent years is a reliable indicator of the growing attitude that "not every life is a life worth living." More and more hospitals are placing DO NOT RESUSCITATE orders on the charts of elderly patients who are subject to cardiac arrest.

Shouldn't a person with a terminal illness be allowed to die with dignity?

A person who is terminally ill should be allowed a natural death. Death is a mysterious and sometimes painful process; and the dying person benefits from preparing for death and from being treated compassionately. Providing medication to relieve pain may have the incidental effect of hastening death, but the intent is to make the terminally ill person comfortable. Medical procedures performed with the sole purpose of keeping a patient from death can be pointless and even cruel. Letting the person die naturally, with caring attention that minimizes pain and alienation, is death with dignity.

The phrase "death with dignity" is frequently used as a soft-sell label for euthanasia. Death with dignity should not be confused with legislation that goes under the name of "Death with Dignity," "Right to Die," or "Natural Death."

Is it really moral to keep alive someone who is little more than a vegetable?

Sad to say, the term *vegetable* is often applied callously or unthinkingly to some of God's more unfortunate human creatures. It suggests that such persons are of about the same importance as the summer crops in the backyard garden.

A person, even if infirm, enfeebled, or unconscious, is a human being. He or she has full rights, vested by God and recognized by the U.S. Constitution, until the moment of death. In terminal sickness, in a comatose state, that person has a right to compassion and loving care, though not necessarily to extraordinary means to prolong his or her life. The much-publicized Karen Quinlan case illustrates that principle well. Karen fell into a coma (a "persistent vegetative state," as neurologists called it) in 1975. More than a year later, she was removed from a respirator. She has remained alive but comatose, receiving necessary care and intravenous feeding.

Neither the use of the term *vegetable* in this context nor the dehumanizing mentality behind it should go unchallenged by those who respect the inherent dignity of the human person.

What makes a life-preserving means 'extraordinary'?

The definition of *extraordinary means* requires constant updating. The key question is whether there is reasonable expectation that the treatment under consideration is likely to benefit the patient to any significant degree. Among factors to be assessed are the pain and distress that the patient will have to suffer, his or her prospects for life and health if the treatment is done, the cost, and other likely consequences for life and health that may cause great inconvenience. What was generally agreed to be "extraordinary" means yesterday may be considered ordinary today; and what is extraordinary today will likely be "ordinary" tomorrow. Respirators, cardiopulmonary resuscitation, and kidney dialysis should probably be considered ordinary means of patient care in the 1980s; but they wouldn't have been regarded that way twenty years earlier.

Wouldn't it be better if those who cannot make a useful contribution to society could be eliminated?

To measure a person only in terms of what he or she can and can't do is cold, utilitarian, and arrogant. It is also an attitude fraught with danger for the physically and mentally handicapped today, as well as for the elderly, who, in the near future, will represent a very high percentage of the total population in the U.S.

Frightening questions arise: Who will be the judge? What will be the criteria for elimination? If today we find that the mentally retarded and handicapped don't measure up, tomorrow the "hardened" criminals will have to go. Will the infirm be next? At the turn of the next century, when the nation's ratio of young to old will have been reduced significantly, what about the elderly? That question might be raised even sooner, for now there needs to be found a solution to the financial crisis facing the Social Security program. Finally, there would be all sorts of "undesirables" whom society might eliminate as "unuseful."

What sort of godless society would evolve if we eliminate all those judged to be "unuseful"? Chances are, few of us would wish to be among the useful survivors.

When is a person considered dead?
The traditional definition holds that life ends when heartbeat stops and respiration ceases. But advances in medical technology make it possible to maintain circulation and respiration artificially, and raise doubts about the adequacy of the traditional definition.

A resolution adopted in 1975 by the American Bar Association states: "For all legal purposes, a human body with irreversible cessation of total brain function, according to usual and customary standards of medical practice, shall be considered dead." This definition attempts to substitute brain death for cessation of circulatory and respiratory functions.

In 1979, the American Medical Association accepted the ABA definition, not as a substitute for, but in addition to the traditional definition. Physicians generally now think death has occurred where there has been a cessation of all three—brain, circulatory, and respiratory functions.

What is the purpose of definition-of-death legislation?
The purpose of definition-of-death legislation is simply to provide statutory guidelines for knowing when death has occurred. However, people have different motives for seeking

such legislation. Some definition-of-death proponents believe that patients are being kept alive when they should be considered dead. They are fond of citing the case of a comatose person whose brain had apparently ceased to function but whose heart and lungs keep working even with no more than ordinary care. Others fear that some definition-of-death advocates are too eager to declare a person dead (as in the example above).

Definition-of-death legislation is also designed to address the larger questions concerning artificial support-systems and organ transplants. In order for an organ transplant to be successful, the surgery must be performed as soon after death as possible. If one physician considered an organ-donor dead when only the circulatory and respiratory functions had ceased, and another looked also for cessation of certain brain functions, and yet another looked for total and irreversible cessation of all brain functions, some surgeries to remove vital organs would have to begin on patients whom some doctors would consider "alive."

Are there any dangers posed by definition-of-death statutes?
Many critics of definition-of-death legislation fear that an ambiguous definition of death could open the door to active euthanasia. Others think that any legislation may amount to an intrusion into the role of the physician. Another critical concern revolves around the understanding of brain death. Some argue that even "total and irreversible cessation of brain function" is still inadequate as a definition of death. They argue that death should be signalled by complete brain death (actual decay of the brain). Others claim that "total and irreversible brain death" is adequate for a valid declaration of legal death, and that definition-of-death laws incorporating this language have actually damaged the pro-euthanasia cause. The issue is complicated. The variations in interpretations of death may seem subtle, but upon those subtleties laws are being legislated with life-and-death consequences.

Since a person has a right to a natural death, wouldn't it be wise to have laws to protect that right?

"Death with dignity" or "natural death" bills have been legislated in several states and proposed in many more. Supporters of such bills do not trust the traditional guidelines, in which the patient makes a decision in consultation with his physician and family. In the case of mentally incompetent patients, proponents of such legislation don't trust the family, in consultation with the physician, to decide "correctly."

Is there a need for death-with-dignity laws? Any person already has the right to reject extraordinary medical treatment. The law requires no previous oral or written statement from the patient. Physicians do not need it for protection against malpractice suits. No physician has ever been found guilty of "failing" to use extraordinary means to preserve life or of prescribing painkilling drugs that may have the incidental effect of hastening death. Some fear that such legislation would complicate the doctor-patient relationship. It may create many more legal questions than it resolves, making a political football of the process of dying.

The 'living will' seems to have much popular support. Is it a good idea?

Living wills are usually provided for in death-with-dignity legislation. Basically, living wills instruct families and physicians as to how medical care should be applied to a person with a terminal illness or after a life-threatening accident. If the patient lacks competence to make a decision, certain people are empowered to decide whether life-sustaining procedures should be maintained.

On the surface, a living will seems to be a good idea. A person's right to decide should be respected. But living wills present some dangers. Doctors may feel compelled to use extraordinary lifesaving means in the absence of such a document, even when there is no reasonable hope for recovery. If this should happen, excessive inconvenience and cost may be incurred by the family of the terminally ill person. On the other hand, physicians of patients with living wills may feel they have no choice but to refrain from using extraordinary means—even against their better judgment.

The living will is executed when a person is healthy. Later, when he or she is struck with a life-threatening illness or accident, his or her feelings about terminal illness and death may be entirely different from the ideas and attitudes of society and of the medical profession. The person empowered to decide on the fate of the patient may also be in different circumstances or of a different mind on the relevant questions later.

Infanticide

What is infanticide?
Infanticide is the intentional killing of an infant. In the wake of ten years or more of legal abortion on demand, infanticide is becoming a variation on the anti-life theme. It shouldn't be surprising. If babies don't count for much inside the womb, why should they be so special after birth?

How extensively is infanticide practiced in the U.S.?
"I know it happens in hospitals throughout the country," said Dr. C. Everett Koop, surgeon general of the Reagan administration, in an interview reported in the June 28, 1982, issue of *U.S. News & World Report*. "The frequency is difficult to assess, but I call it infanticide."

The frequency is difficult to assess because you'll never find hospitals recording infanticide as the cause of death. However, in a highly publicized case in a New Haven, Connecticut, hospital in 1973, 43 of 299 deaths in a special-care nursery were caused by the withholding of treatment. Usually the victims of infanticide are children with Down's syndrome (mongolism), a majority of whom, if treated early, can achieve "significant" personal development. Yet, according to a survey of pediatricians conducted in Massachusetts in 1977, fifty-one percent said that they would not recommend lifesaving surgery for a Down's syndrome baby with intestinal blockage.

How does a hospital practice infanticide?
Because of the way hospital records are kept, it is not known how frequently each method is used, but the withholding of lifesaving treatment, starvation, and dehydration are the usual methods of infanticide. Lethal drugs are also employed, but their use is even more difficult to trace. There is every reason to believe that the situation described in an article in the Hartford *Courant*, June 14, 1981, is repeated in many U.S. hospitals:

> *In some cases, doctors at Yale-New Haven [Hospital] have helped parents give their defective infants lethal drug overdoses, two doctors there said. . . . In some of the cases . . . parents approached doctors about the possibility of overdose. Other times . . . doctors suggested the option, assuring parents they would sign the death certificate, no questions asked.*
>
> *The parents . . . ended their infants' lives with morphine or phenobarbital prescribed by the doctors and usually dissolved in a baby bottle.*

Is infanticide legal in the U.S.?
Infanticide is illegal in every state in the U.S. Physicians and parents can be prosecuted for murder, involuntary manslaughter, child abuse, or neglect for withholding ordinary medical care from seriously impaired newborns.

Because deaths of defective newborns are usually attributed to some medical cause, most cases are never brought to public attention. The Baby Doe case of April 1982, in Bloomington, Indiana, is a rare exception. Baby Doe was born April 9 with Down's syndrome and a correctable defect that prevented food from reaching his stomach. He was condemned to die at a hearing because, in the words of the judge, "the possibility of a minimally adequate quality of life was nonexistent." Treatment, food, and water were withheld, and Baby Doe died six days later.

Have any physicians or parents been prosecuted for killing defective newborns?
No. In 1981, however, the parents and the doctor of Siamese twins born in Danville, Illinois, were charged with attempted murder. The charges were later dismissed. (The twins, born May 5, 1981, were surgically separated about a year later, in spite of repeated diagnoses that they could not survive such surgery.)

A number of reasons have been suggested for the reluctance to prosecute in cases of infanticide. The care (or lack of care) of defective newborns has been left exclusively in the hands of physicians and parents. Some prosecutors are supportive of infanticide and unwilling to go against their own sympathies. Also, cases of infanticide generally are difficult to identify.

How do those involved in infanticide justify their actions?
They argue that a physician or a parent is not obliged to provide more than ordinary care to a newborn child. They then go on to say that any care provided a newborn with major defects should be considered extraordinary.

Ordinary care, properly understood, includes nourishment, surgeries, treatments, and medicines that offer reasonable hope of benefit and that can be provided without excessive pain, cost, or inconvenience. Treatments deserve to be called extraordinary when they offer little hope of benefit or cannot be provided without excessive pain, cost, or other inconvenience.

Another justification offered by proponents of infanticide is that often medical care cannot reasonably be expected substantially to extend the life of the defective newborn. Since the child's death is considered imminent anyway, the denial of medical care, it is argued, should not be considered the cause of death.

Those who favor infanticide in the case of a defective newborn at times argue that the withholding of treatment spares the child prolonged physical suffering and also spares the family considerable psychological, economic, and social stress.

Aren't the arguments in defense of infanticide humane and reasonable?

Some hold that any medical care of a defective newborn is to be regarded as extraordinary. That opinion can only follow from the premise that the lives of defective newborns are of no value and that they should be regarded as nonhumans. Such a premise provides the rationalization for slavery, Nazi and Soviet discrimination against Jews and others, and the increasingly common genocidal practices of our contemporary world.

Then too, is the avoidance of pain, suffering, and inconvenience a higher value than life itself? It is consistent that proponents of infanticide would follow such an ethic. But a world unwilling to confront pain, suffering, and inconvenience would also be a world devoid of care, compassion, and courage.

The arguments invariably neglect crucial considerations. Would it be the child's desire to be killed? Have we the right to play God? Are we not all less than perfect?

But isn't a severely impaired child incapable of living a meaningful human life?

"Meaningful human life" is one of the buzz phrases that are constantly bandied about by those who see infanticide as desirable. Invariably it follows from the "quality of life" ethic, which calculates the value of a person's life according to its supposed usefulness.

In fact, the quality of life of the defective newborn can be quite high. Such a child may hunger to live his life to the full and derive much happiness in the process. He may also have much to give. A mother says of her child born with spina bifida: "My son is not quite twelve. He can read and write the Russian and Greek alphabets and is learning Hebrew,

Czech and Serbo-Croatian. His reading skill is on college level, his abstract reasoning in the superior range . . . ." Yes, there was "stress, sorrow and anguish," but "these children also bring joy, delight and fulfillment, together with a wonderful opportunity to grow emotionally and spiritually, far more than is allowed the 'average parent.'. . . We love our son, and though we have suffered with him through trials his handicap has brought to us all, so we have grown, matured and, I hope, become better human beings because of those trials" (*The Human Life Review*, Summer 1982).

There is no such thing as meaningless human life. Life is created with purpose. It is through our own blindness or arrogance that we deny meaning to the life of any human being.

Isn't it unfair to expect parents to decide what to do about a brain-damaged newborn?

It is natural for every pair of parents to expect their newborn to be a "perfect" baby. As pregnancy approaches its completion, they are full of excitement and anticipation. So it is also natural that the parents of a severely impaired child experience shock, grief, guilt, shame, and despair.

Quite naturally, the stricken parents often experience anxiety over the anticipated hardships a defective newborn will cause. How will these problems affect their marriage? their family? their financial future?

All that is quite a burden for parents. They need support and assistance from the medical community and from the community at large. What they don't need is to be left alone or offered the quick and easy solution of "getting rid of it," as if the child were nothing more significant than a bad dream.

What should be the role of the physician and medical staff in counseling parents of a defective newborn?

The first thing medical personnel can offer is sensitivity to the parents. As the shock of having brought a defective new-born into the world sets in, the bewildered parents will first look to them for support.

Second, medical authorities need to provide a clear assessment of the child's condition. They need to answer a great many questions, including some that the parents may be too confused even to ask. What treatments are necessary for the child's life or desirable for the child's welfare? Is there reasonable hope of benefit? What are the likely consequences of treatment?

Third, with the knowledge the physicians possess, they can then assist the parents to see what course of surgery or corrective treatments is best. At times, the best decision may be to take no action other than to alleviate pain. Some children are simply born dying.

Finally, the medical staff can teach parents how to provide love and care to their impaired newborn, and to see also that the child is God-given.

Should a physician recommend denial of food and sustenance to a severely impaired newborn?

This is a question that physicians once would not have dignified with a response. Today it is asked, and some physicians are answering it affirmatively.

"Nontreatment," spoken of as if it were a specific form of treatment, has become the semantic end-run around the entire infanticide question. Infanticide is illegal, so to give it a label of acceptability and legality, nontreatment is called treatment. Starving a human being, regardless of that person's state of being, is morally reprehensible. It is totally indefensible as a means of "treatment" of a defective newborn. To starve a child is to kill that child deliberately—and cruelly.

Isn't giving a lethal drug to a severely impaired newborn more merciful than starving him?

Administering a lethal drug is, in a sense, more merciful, and perhaps less cowardly. Death by starvation is slow agony.

But a lethal injection still kills a human being. By administering death through drugs rather than by starvation, one merely kills less cruelly. Regardless of the method, the act is one of killing.

What are 'wrongful life' cases?

Years ago, physicians and others whose task was to care for a child would occasionally be sued by parents for the "wrongful death" of their child. The legal principle involved alleged negligence or incompetence on the part of the medical or supervisory personnel leading to a child's preventable death. Today, that situation has a sad variation called "wrongful life." Parents are suing physicians because a child they didn't want is *alive!*

There are three varieties of wrongful-life cases. There is the wrongful-conception case, in which a physician is held liable for failure of a sterilization procedure; the wrongful-birth case, in which the physician allegedly failed to inform the parents of possible birth defects—knowledge that would have persuaded them to abort the child; and the wrongful-life case, in which parents, suing on behalf of their handicapped child, hold the physician liable for allowing that child to be born.

Shouldn't a physician be held liable in wrongful-life and wrongful-birth cases?

To say so would amount to suggesting that doctors *ought to be* instruments of death as much as instruments of healing. To agree that doctors deserve to be legally punished *because* an impaired child has life amounts to agreeing that the "less than perfect" have no right to membership in the human race. They are deemed so worthless that parents who are "stuck" with them can sue because their handicapped children are alive.

In 1981, a wrongful-life claim was denied by the California Court of Appeals. In this case, a suit was brought on behalf of a child born deaf because of a genetic defect. The grounds were that her birth should have been prevented. The parents had been assured by a doctor that their older child's deafness was not hereditary; but that diagnosis was reversed after the birth of the second child, who was also deaf. In 1980, another California Court of Appeals ruled that a right did exist to sue for wrongful life. Also in 1981, in another case, a United States Court of Appeals recognized a wrongful-birth claim. And in Illinois, a physician was held liable by an appellate court for damages in a wrongful-conception case.

Successful prosecution of wrongful-life cases will pressure physicians to become medical detectives whose responsibilities ultimately will be to declare war on defective children in the womb. If this principle is carried to its logical extreme, a physician would face a difficult dilemma: go along, and live by the principle, or risk being unable to obtain malpractice insurance. But to go along with this anti-life orientation that declares war on the imperfect would effectively end his practice, at least in the traditional sense of medicine as the art of healing.

Is there any relationship between infanticide and abortion?
Yes. First, they both kill. Abortion (also called feticide) kills the unborn. Infanticide kills the already born. If the unborn child can be killed, why not the child after birth?

In the U.S., an unborn child can be killed for any reason whatsoever. At present, a born child is allowed to be killed (albeit illegally) if he possesses some serious impairment.

Formerly, when abortion was illegal in the U.S., some women did obtain abortions with the assistance of some in the medical profession. Those abortions were overlooked. Then there arose a movement advocating the legalization of abortion, in one state, then another, and so on—for the "hard cases" of rape, incest, or prognosis of impaired child. Proponents of abortion continued to take advantage of such legal approval of abortion till the door was fully opened to abortion-on-demand (the Supreme Court decision of 1973).

Compare the case of infanticide. It is now illegal, but newborns are now being killed with the support of some in the medical profession. These killings are overlooked. There is now a movement afoot to open the door wider, to legalize infanticide in cases of severely impaired newborns (the "hard cases"). If this movement has its will, the door will open wider, perhaps till it is wide open.

Absurd? Perhaps. But who had thought, a few decades ago, that abortion would be legal to the present extent in the U.S.? Some would justify abortion if the child is the "wrong" sex or might "interrupt" his parents' life. Even if a woman simply does not "want" the child, she may now abort him legally. The same reasons that were used to justify killing the unborn can be used to defend killing children already born.

Bibliography

The following are the main sources used in preparing this book, and can be recommended as sources of additional information about the topics discussed in this book.

Billings, Evelyn, and Ann Westmore, *The Billings Method* (N.Y.: Random House, 1980).

Burtchaell, James Tunstead, C.S.C., *Rachel Weeping* (Kansas City: Andrews & McMeel, 1982).

Connery, John, S.J., *Abortion: The Development of the Roman Catholic Perspective* (Chicago: Loyola University Press, 1977).

Flanagan, Geraldine L., *The First Nine Months of Life* (N.Y.: Simon and Schuster, 1965).

Ganz, Richard L., ed., *Thou Shalt Not Kill* (New Rochelle, N.Y.: Arlington House, 1978).

Hilgers, Thomas W., and Dennis J. Horan, eds., *Abortion and Social Justice* (N.Y.: Sheed & Ward, 1972).

Hilgers, Thomas W., et al., eds., *New Perspectives on Human Abortion* (Frederick, Md.: University Publications of America, 1981).

Horan, Dennis J., and David Mall, eds., *Death, Dying, and Euthanasia* (Washington, D.C.: University Publications of America, 1977).

Mall, David, and Walter F. Watts, eds., *The Psychological Aspects of Abortion* (Washington, D.C.: University Publications of America, 1979).

McCarthy, Donald G., and Edward J. Bayer, eds., *Handbook on Critical Life Issues* (St. Louis: Pope John Center, 1982).

Nathanson, Bernard N., *Aborting America* (Garden City: Doubleday, 1979).

Noonan, John T., Jr., *The Morality of Abortion* (Cambridge: Harvard University Press, 1972).

Noonan, John T., Jr., *A Private Choice* (N.Y.: Free Press, 1979).

Powell, John, s.j., *Abortion: The Silent Holocaust* (Allen, Texas: Argus Communications, 1981).

Ramsey, Paul, *The Ethics of Fetal Research* (New Haven: Yale University Press, 1975).

Wardle, Lynn D., and Mary Anne Wood, *A Lawyer Looks at Abortion* (Provo: Brigham Young University, 1982).

Weber, Leonard J., *Who Shall Live?* (N.Y.: Paulist, 1976).

Willke, Dr. and Mrs. J. C., *Handbook on Abortion* (Cincinnati: Hayes, 1979).

The Human Life Review. Quarterly review published by The Human Life Foundation, 150 East 35th Street, New York, N.Y. 10016.

National Right to Life News. Biweekly publication of the National Right to Life Committee, 419 7th Street, Suite 402, Washington, D.C. 20004.

Studies in Law and Medicine and *Lex Vitae.* Publications of Americans United for Life, 230 N. Michigan Avenue, Suite 915, Chicago, Illinois 60601.